REVIEWS

An inspiring firsthand testimony of God's grace, faithfulness, and loving kindness in the lives of a mother, her mother who nurtured her through thick and thin, and her daughters. Truly those who fear and honor the Lord are blessed in the end. The touching return of a prodigal gives hope that kindness and prayer will win in the end. God is the Promise Keeper indeed.

Goldie Chong
Counselor
Australia

The writer carefully and prayerfully weaved the uncertain minefield of conflicting generations through the intertwining fabric of Chinese culture and Christian values. While sharing the agony of three generations of Chinese women, she managed to trace the goodness and grace of our God who is no one's debtor. He is the Keeper of the biblical promise that God will honor those who honor Him.

Chong Kwong Tek
Doctor and Pastor
Australia

An amazing story well told, as real and as dramatic as it can be, even if written incognito. Reading *Grace On Time—The Story of Sian*, we are immediately transported into the broad world of the overseas Chinese diaspora, yet are immediately pulled back into intimate, personal accounts that resonate with our personal, family, church, and national life.

Soo Ewe Jin
Senior Journalist
Malaysia

GRACE on TIME

The Story of Sian
Overseas Chinese Women in Transition

MEIDELI SAW

PARTRIDGE
A Penguin Random House Company

To order additional copies of this book, contact
Toll Free 800 101 2657 (Singapore)
Toll Free 1 800 81 7340 (Malaysia)
orders.singapore@partridgepublishing.com

www.partridgepublishing.com/singapore

Dedicated to
The Provider of
Grace upon Grace

Acknowledgment

The author is grateful to her siblings who kick-started the process of writing of *Grace on Time* and for those who took time to read through the manuscript and gave reviews and useful comments for editing. A special thanks is also extended to the publishing team of Trafford Publishing who delivered this book into the world.

Note

Though this book is based on a true story, the names of people, places and events have been changed to provide privacy in a small–BIG world where personal space has largely been intruded for better or for worse. Any identification of persons mentioned in the text is accidental.

Contents

Prologue

8 March 2012

I am a creature of intuition and feeling. Writing this novel will exhilarate me a lot. After an eight-year hiatus of the writer's block, words and sentences seem to be flowing rapidly out of my mind and heart again. My several previous attempts to bring myself to write a story have failed miserably, despite my having written, produced, and distributed several titles on a variety of topics in my homeland since 1992. There must be a reason for this. You may yet be the benefactor of something meaningful and beautiful. It is said that a seed must die in order for it to become a shoot. Where will this lead me? I shall pray, wait and see.

Furthermore, I find it rather strange that I do not know how to invent a story about people. I have heard firsthand tales of thousands of people in five continents, yet I am at a loss to write fiction. Nevertheless, I do know how to retell stories of real people in the real dramas of life. That is why I am writing now. If you see yourself in any of these characters or scenes and events, so that the reading becomes therapeutic for you, I would be rewarded as a writer. I would be even more rewarded if these tales put a handle to the door of forgiveness and reconciliation in your personal, family, church, or national life.

A writer is only a scribe. She is like an artist who paints her objects with words; she is also like a weaver who brings together the threads of human relationships into a more meaningful whole with which readers may identify, be healed and be a blessing to others. By writing, she wishes to make some sense out of the nonsense of the lives of her characters. Truly, if the world is like a stage and all its citizens are players, then please allow me to draw back the curtains of a human community for us to view, to listen and to ponder afresh what words may reveal in our own hearts.

Sometimes, I wonder, from the other side of the world from the United States, what could have happened *if* those responsible for the September 11 tragedy had been declared *forgiven* at a personal level yet brought to *public accountability*? Would not that have been a timely open door to let the world experience the reality of the truth of God's grace as never before? Is there hope in anything else apart from grace, anyway? Would not the hope through forgiveness and reconciliation, with whoever our enemies might be, reverberate through the universe? There is a marginal hypothetical possibility that it could have happened in a dramatic and yet unintentional manner. That is history now but lessons gleaned on hindsight can help ordinary people like us who come from a multitude of nations and backgrounds. Reflections can help us in our current interactions with one another as fellow broken men and women in a damaged world hopefully, on the mend.

Before we venture into chapter 1, I would like to mention three points:

First, the overseas Chinese diaspora spans the far corners of the world. For example, I was pleasantly surprised to dine in a posh Chinese restaurant owned by a mainland Chinese boss who employed local black African waiters, together with cheong sam (a Chinese long tight dress) clad Chinese waitresses, right in Cape Town, in October 2010. Indeed, I felt good and happy to be able to treat my new young black female undergraduate African friend to a full Chinese lunch in South Africa. A Chinese is often proud to be one, no matter how many other worldviews they may have collected on the way since birth. They did not choose to be born such, but, having been born alive, most of them accept their temporal genetic identity wherever they happen to land.

Secondly, having studied, lived and worked in five out of six continents in the last six decades, I count it a privilege to be able to sit back and try to put all that I have experienced in a logical form so that it makes sense to my feeble mind. What better way is there to do this than to write a novel based on true stories?

Thirdly, I have tried to fill in my wide cultural gaps by reading biographies or non-fiction novels and watching movies set in various natural-cultural-religious-political context. This sharpens my insight into human relationships and enables me to accept much of my observation of common human nature of the people of the world. The best movies are those with which we can identify. This means that what happens in plots of movies, though coined by scriptwriters, are events which actually happen all the time or will do so again.

One of my husband's Caucasian Canadian friends once made this observation: that, having lectured and mingled with Chinese college students for decades in the UK and Canada, he used to think that Caucasian kids were dysfunctional till he got to know Chinese students! I leave you to make your personal deductions. However, if you are currently having relational problems with some Chinese friends, please do not forsake them yet. Patience is a virtue for all, irrespective of race, religion, culture and of being of the east or west. I, too, will benefit if you practice this virtue in your reading because I happen to be born and bred a Chinese, even though overseas.

Thanks for reading.

With warm regards
Meideli
Malaysia

The Extended Family of Ah Li and Sian

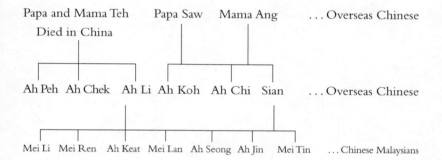

Papa and Mama Teh   Papa Saw   Mama Ang   . . . Overseas Chinese
Died in China

Ah Peh   Ah Chek   Ah Li   Ah Koh   Ah Chi   Sian   . . . Overseas Chinese

Mei Li   Mei Ren   Ah Keat   Mei Lan   Ah Seong   Ah Jin   Mei Tin   . . . Chinese Malaysians

Chapter 1

A Daughter in Early Twentieth Century Singapore

Singapore 1913

At the dawn of the twentieth century, Papa Saw and Mama Ang left Fujian Province in South China for better days in Singapore with their twelve-year daughter, Ah Chi, and ten-year-old son, Ah Koh. Excitement was in the air as their junk anchored near enough to the old-fashioned jetty at the busy British port of Singapore. Having found a place to stay, the *SinKhek's* (literally meaning *new guest or new arrival* in a Southern China dilect, Hokkien) young family settled down to a new livelihood among other overseas Chinese who came to South East Asia to look for their fortunes. Work was easy to find, and the four nuclear family members lived relatively happy days, despite missing their extended family back home in their village in China.

Without modern medical advice on birth control, Papa Saw and Mama Ang soon had another girl, Sian. Though having one more mouth to feed, everyone rejoiced over the little baby who soon turned one year-old. Sian was a symbol of the family's fresh start in life on alien ground. Whereas Ah Koh helped Papa

Saw to bring in cash, Ah Chi babysat and played with Sian every day. What is a better gift to a little girl than to have a big sister to dote on her; what is a better gift for a big sister than to have a real life little sister to fuss over; definitely they were better than dolls which the family could not afford anyway! Mama Ang was home minister with joy!

However, the serene family's life was interrupted when, another three years later, a letter arrived from the Saw village. Papa Saw's distant cousin sister's son needed a wife back home. Ah Chi was the only one old enough to make a match. Hence, very soon, big sister Ah Chi was separated from little sister Sian *forever*. Both shed tears of good-bye as Sian watched big sister's junk silently sailing out of the harbor to disappear into the distant horizon. That was Sian's first experience of grief, though she could not understand what was going on. How she prayed to her mother's gods, how she promised to be a good girl so that she could have her big sister back. Mama Ang was just too caught up with family chores for songs and games. Papa Saw and big brother were boys! Boys and girls did very different things those days. Boys were free to roam the streets but not girls; births of boys were celebrated but not of girls. *Why?* Born into such a tradition, Sian simply accepted the fact of the situation and never questioned why.

Today's women, however, want to know why this was so.

Traditional Chinese families use surnames (family names), which were passed from generation to generation through males only. Once married, the wife and children inherited the surname of the husband and father respectively. Until married, a woman was known as her father's daughter; if her father died, she was her eldest brother's sister. When she married, she was her husband's wife; if her husband died, she would be known as her son's mother. Therefore, in traditional Chinese culture, a woman had no identity of her own. She was never accepted for herself. Her identity lay in her father, brother, husband and son. Do you now understand why a wife in such a family structure prayed for, cried for, and reluctantly allowed the husband to have a concubine in order to have at least one son? Then, the concubine's son would officially become the wife's son to uplift the latter's dignity. Blessed was the mother who had at least one son though, emotionally, she longed for at least a daughter to identify with her! Not blessed was the mother if she were that concubine for her son might be taken away from her to call another woman "*Mama.*"

Sian was fortunate to have an older brother born before her to reduce some of the misfortune of being a girl. How big sister and big brother loved her. Big brother often piggybacked her whenever he could. He was the suave trishaw-puller and she the pretty damsel, who hailed him in the street. She would pay him for the ride with her collection of used bottle caps when they reached her "doorstep." Sometimes, he was the sedan chair carrier while she was the princess needing to rush home or Mama would be worried! All these he did to cheer up little sister since big sister left to get married, the best lot for any woman of those days. At times, he would race her up and down the narrow staircase of their small double-story house or carried her piggybacked again. Her screams of laughter and giggles kept him going, even when he was tired, till one evening . . . big brother missed a step, and Sian tumbled down every other step till she landed with a bump at the bottom of the squeaky stairs.

Silence.

Little Sian screamed and cried in puzzling pain. What happened? Mama Ang left every utensil in the dark kitchen and ran to find out what had happened. On seeing her baby on the floor, she scooped her up with her strong arms and hugged her tightly. When Sian's cries became sobs, Mama put her gently on her back on the dining table to examine her fragile frame. Was every part of baby intact? She seemed to be in one piece—no cuts, no lumps.

After a few moments, she sat Sian down on her high chair for dinner with the rest of the family. Yummy pork porridge would calm her down and distract her from her traumatic experience. *But,* horror of horrors, she screamed all over again as if someone was beating her. She could not sit as her left buttock was so sensitively tender. She could not be consoled till Mama lifted her from the chair so that her left hip and leg were off weight bearing. Then she noticed that her left leg was shorter than her right and she could not straighten it completely! What went wrong? It was an emergency; they called Mr. Gan, the Chinese medicine man who had also emigrated from China. Without the easy availability of radiographers then, he would be the best diagnostician and physician.

On checking Sian's frail body, he shook his head. That got Mama worried!

"Mr. Gan, what's wrong? How is my daughter? Any broken bones or sprains?"

He slowly replied,

"Mrs. Ang, I am afraid your daughter's hip bone is dislocated. Her left thigh bone has been pushed beyond her hip joint."

Madam Ang was relieved that no bone was broken, not so serious after all.

"But, Madam Ang, she may have a limp for the rest of her life."

"But why, Mr. Gan?" she panicked once more as her head felt unsteady.

"I will do my best to help her. Her hip joint is not fully formed yet. If we do not move her thigh bone too much and keep it in a natural

position, her growing hip and pelvic bones may come together normally in years to come."

"Years?!" Mama repeated his words and cried helplessly.

"My beautiful baby, what will happen to you?" she mourned. Then, realizing she had to be strong for her daughter, she dried her eyes with the end of her long sleeve and controlled herself.

"Thank you, Mr. Gan, please do what you can for my precious daughter," she pleaded.

What was the treatment for Sian? After an initial trial of failed manipulation to set the head of the thigh bone into the unseen joint, for months on end, her upper thighs were tied together with outstretched legs so that the dislocated thigh bone would not slip back into the gap in her hip. The right leg thus acted as a splint to immobilize the left. Mama Ang made the strong bandage from a wide piece of cotton cloth that she had bought to make a new shirt for Papa in the coming Chinese New Year.

After three months, Sian was allowed to sit up after her thighs and legs were untied and her thighs slowly and gradually bent enough for her to sit painlessly. Internal bleeding and edema in the hip joint had caused much acute pain. But once that subsided, the initial pain disappeared. However, poor Sian cringed in pain once more when the physician gently moved her left hip joint for her to sit, in the hope of the head of the left femur slipping into place. Unused ligaments and muscles tend to get stiff and unlocking that stiffness needed a hard-heartedness and a determined hand as the patient resisted movement due to the excruciating pain that inevitably accompanied such a movement. Just as unused locks need to be lubricated before use, so do unused human joints, except that in this case, the fluid was naturally produced within the joint. With regular exercise, Sian would walk again soon if the head of bone did not slip out of place once more.

There was no way for the physician to view the structure of the bones without modern technology. X-rays taken decades later revealed that the left femoral head was not only malformed because it did not grow in its original immature socket, but it was located behind the natural left hip joint. This meant that the femoral head was held strong enough adjacent to the pelvic bone only by surrounding muscles and tendons. The future was rather bleak. What if she became weaker in old age? Would the muscles still be strong enough to hold the bones in the hip joint together? At that stage, no assurance could be given. It was wiser for Mama not to think too far ahead but to take things one day at a time.

From the day of the accident, big brother took upon himself to carry Sian wherever she wanted to go till she could walk without pain again. This took more than a year. Often, late in the night, when the rest of the family was asleep, big brother wept silently, being angry at himself for missing a step. How was he going to remove the guilt for having caused his beloved sister to limp for the rest of her life, if she was not healed completely? It might also lower her chances of marrying a handsome, rich, and well-educated man.

For the rest of her otherwise healthy life, Sian walked with a limp as her left leg became functionally shorter than her right. No young lady wanted that indeed.

Thus Sian was crippled for the rest of her life. She could not run around with their neighbors' kids for months. Each evening, she would wait for big brother to play with her. He could not throw caution to the wind anymore. Often, he would show her his picture and school songbooks and taught her to draw and sing by memory. At times, he would let her color the black and white art book he bought with his pocket money to cheer her up and to educate her a bit. Educate? Why?

This is because Papa Saw refused to allow Sian to attend school. What was the use of being educated? She too would be married off. That would be a blessing to her and to her parents-in-law. For the time being, all she needed to learn were household tasks, which would increase her eligibility to be match made to a man of good standing and diligence among their friends. How proud her parents would be!

As Sian grew into the pubertal years, she knew that her gait would be a minus point to her parents' matchmaking effort. Therefore, secretly, she planned to learn how to read and write from a private teacher the moment a tiny gap appeared in the doorway to the outside world.

"I want to read and write like big brother," she promised herself. *"It is so unfair that he can go to school and I can't just because I am a girl! I never asked to be a girl!"* muttered Sian angrily as she cried to sleep one night. She thought no one heard her but big brother did. He had been out of the house more, much more, and he knew of many young ladies who were educated at home because they had rich parents who could afford to pay for private tutors. He vowed to help little sister become like those ladies when he could work to support her. Then Papa could not object as he did not have to think that his money spent on her education would be wasted if she were to get married. He too fell asleep but with a hopeful smile on his caring face.

When Sian was about seven years old, Papa had an affair with an acquaintance. When Mama suspected something was amiss through his body language, she wanted the truth out of him. Initially, Papa denied his extramarital relationship. Then he admitted it but asserted that it was only a fling, though that was bad enough for a loyal wife. After frequent questioning and checking of his outside activities by Sian, Papa confessed that he had a second woman in his life. However, he adamantly refused to give her up. What could Mama do?

After pouring out her pain, anger, and confusion to Madam Ng, the teacher she met in the market months ago, Mama Ang felt better. She struggled as she planned to run away reluctantly from the love of her life, Papa Saw. Though a *sinKhek* in a foreign land, there was no way she could accept sharing her husband with another woman. Yes, in China, it was an accepted traditional Chinese custom to have more than one wife. However, in British Singapore, she knew enough of modern Singaporean family life to learn that she did not have to tolerate her husband's taking a second wife. The British law would protect her! Somehow, she would reject his polygamous stand. But should she take both children with her, one, or none?

Sian was too young to be left with Papa. She would never let another woman be her Mama any way! Ah Koh was seventeen, in school and mature. Maybe it would be better for Papa to bring him up. He was also old enough to understand her pains and would forgive her. When she had found a job and settled down in Malaya, she could always see him again. Hence, though she was anxious over parting with her caring and good son, she had to leave him behind. Of course, Ah Koh pleaded to go with them. He would miss them so much. Big sister had left, but Sian was his beloved sister and playmate. Now Sian and Mama Ang were leaving so quickly too. Who could he chat with and lean on in times of sorrow or joy? Papa was either too busy working or, since he knew the other woman, too busy entertaining her! He got irritable each time Ah Koh tried to persuade him to spend more time at home. He must not get into his way. Sorrow and anger were thus pent up in young Ah Koh's heart. He had to survive without Mama Ang to love and care for him.

One night, Papa did not return to sleep in the house. Mama quickly packed her bags and hid in Madam Ng's home, with Sian trailing beside her. She dared not even confide in her son her destination for fear of Papa forcing the information out of him. Ah Koh had been prepared that one day, if Mama and Sian could not be found, he must look to Madam Ng for help of any sort. They embraced and assured each other of their mutual undivided loyalty as a family. Ah Koh must obey Papa and take care of him whenever Papa needed him. Mama would be so proud of him as a good son. Very reluctantly, precocious Ah Koh agreed.

When morning light dawned, Madam Ng drove her to the Malayan Railway Station at Tanjung Pagar and saw them off on the express train to the northern town of Taiping in the state of Perak. Madam Ng had a good teacher friend over there. She would shelter them till Mama could support Sian and herself. She had some cash with her and would be fine for a few weeks. Of course, Madam Ng hoped that Mama Ang's family would be reconciled soon. A broken family was bad for anyone. But being on your own in a strange land made it worse! Yes, she empathized with Mama Ang and helped her where she could. How true was the saying, *"A friend in need is a friend indeed"*!

"Thankfully, I am single and am spared from such a tragic shock," Ng pondered within herself.

But then, singlehood had its own troubles as the society of those days did not easily accept singlehood as an option or gift. When a girl reached her late teens or a boy his early twenties and was still single, aunts, uncles, well-intentioned friends and busybodies would try their best to marry them off. If the young refused, they might be regarded as odd, having a secret illness or promiscuous. Sometimes, just to shut them up, the young married a wrong spouse.

"Aiyahhh, never mind-lah . . . just marry to please them-lah!" some would say.

This attitude sometimes caused a severe lack of love for the future spouse who had hope of a happy married life. However, many did begin to love one another after marriage. Indeed, as an African pastor once taught, *"Love is a feeling to be learned . . ."*

Mama Saw stared at the jungles of Malaya as the train rocked on the old-time tracks. She really wanted the three of them, Sian, Ah Koh, and herself to be together and leave Papa Saw to carry on with his foolish antics. Her son would be strong for the two ladies. However, neither was it easy to feed another mouth. Son would be better off with his father. Already, fearful that Ah Koh would be influenced by his mother's anger against him, even before Mama and Sian left, Papa had arranged for him to live with his Singaporean boss who would provide for Ah Koh's food, lodging, and education. Ah Koh did not like that at all, but he had no choice but to submit to his father's orders. That was how many traditional Chinese children grew up.

Why did an illiterate woman take this difficult step of no return? Were they not relatively safe in Singapore and were well fed and clothed? Strange to our modern ears, I believe that even then, the urge to be treated fairly was already naturally ingrained in a woman's nature. Loyalty in marriage was also a natural expectation. The Creator must have punched the same chop into all born woman or *man*. Ancient women did not really need twenty-first century secularized individualistic women to teach them to burn the bra as a symbol of their need to fight for equal rights with men. They needed only be simply women, equal in status with men in the eyes of the Creator, though they may have differing personalities and roles in the family and in this huge world which had space for all. Hence, Mama Ang must have felt it better to be independent though poor and living under the stigma of being a single mother than to live under the roof of an unfaithful husband. She felt that her neighbor's talk, about wives not minding to share their husbands with other women, only played into the hands of selfish men. If society accepted polygamy or sharing of spouses, where then was their womanly human dignity to be the only wife and sexual partner of their spouse? Physical union was a symbol of the high calling to the exclusive oneness and commitment between a man and his wife; in this commitment, their children would be secure.

Mama worked hard to support little Sian and herself. Papa could take care of their son till he too could find his own fortune. The thought occurred that she might not meet Ah Koh again. For now, the thought of missing her son tore at her heart as the old train ricketted on its tracks.

In later days, daughter Sian could not recall the details of those traumatic years. She had Mama's love, anyway. However, having to be ripped off a sister and now, a brother and father, had left a haunting wound in her heart. She missed them but did not know how to express her suppressed grief. She understood the tension enough, though, that she must not mention Papa Saw's name to Mama Ang. She must be good so that Mama Ang would be happy. What could a child do? Better to obey Mama and start making friends all over again in their new home. What would it be like? Would there be friends of her age?

Chapter 2

Sian

Taiping, Malaya 1920

Due to poverty, Mama Ang and her daughter rented a simple small room from the landlord Sim. It was nearby to the Taiping Anglo Chinese School (ACS), which belonged to the local Chinese Church. After Mama Ang received permission to sell her cakes at the school canteen, Ah Hoo Ma, a Malaysian *nonya* [a lady nurtured in a gentle blend of Malay, Chinese, Thai, Java and European cultures in Malaya. She practiced what was called *the Peranakan culture* of the *Babas* (men) and Nonyas (women)] who taught English at the ACS, became her trusted friend. Ah Hoo Ma often ordered the cakes Mama Ang made and Sian sold.

Soon, Ah Hoo Ma, the extrovert popular lady in town, understood the hardship of the mother child team eking an income to live on. They did not complain or long for others' material wealth. Mama Ang also did the laundry for richer folks in town while Sian daily cycled to and fro to collect dirty linen and return the washed and ironed ones. They were so poor that, for most days, their daily meal consisted of plain thin porridge with hot soup made up of repeatedly boiled salt fish bones. Today's health conscious global people may not fathom how they did not suffer from malnutrition. God knew their lowly position and must have worked a miracle in their bodies. Nevertheless, mother and daughter felt happy and safe among new and caring friends who not only taught them how to *fish* by training them in basic business skills, but also gave them *fish"* (e.g. rice, canned milk powder, tins of milo, and new clothes for fast-growing Sian) during festival times. These were rare gifts rallied on them, things taken for granted when home with Papa Saw.

In her quiet moments after an evening bath, Sian recalled better times with Papa Saw and Big Brother Ah Koh. They used to celebrate each Chinese New Year period with extra food, drinks, new shoes, and new smartly feminine *samfu* (Chinese-styled paired long pants and blouse) or with Singapore-styled westernized dresses and ribbons. However, such reminiscence must be put aside it was useless longing for them now. Self-pity would not help her as the only daughter of a now-single mother. Put on a smile (and Sian's sweet smile endeared her to all) and work hard. Hopefully, she would meet a fine young man and have a home of her own one day. She could then give Mama Ang a better life. For now, as she grew into her late teens, this thought flicked past her mind . . .

"What if my husband also becomes unfaithful to me? Better not think too much; time to deliver the fresh laundry. It is enough to have good friends now!" pondered Sian to herself.

How did Ah Hoo Ma and others become trusted friends over the months and years?

Well, a local *towkay* (Hokkien for boss) had a hunchback son who was of marriageable age. Tuberculosis, a stigma in local pre-antibiotic days, had eaten into his spine. Now, this young man liked the lovely and fair Sian a lot. Daily, he watched her cycle past his mansion to and from her home to sell the popular *nonya kueh* (*nonya*cakes) which Mama Ang steamed. His family had even pretended to need Mama's laundry service in the hope of matching Sian to their son. However, their hope evaporated because neither Sian nor her mother liked their son, Ah Huat, rich though they were. So Ah Huat pined for Sian while Sian made every attempt to avoid meeting him on the road each day.

Then, horror of horrors, one evening, as Sian cycled near a quiet spot, Ah Huat jumped out from a bush and lurched at her. He pulled her down and tried to molest her so that other suitors would reject her. Hopefully, she would then agree to marry him. Her manipulated immorality would balance up his having a hunchback. An unthinkable silly way of getting a bride by modern day terms and a selfish act by any terms!

But Sian struggled and fought back. She ran into the local Chinese Church! The pastor's family lived on the church grounds in a house called a parsonage. She banged its door and yelled for help in desperation. The door opened, and there stood her Mama's friend, Ah Hoo Ma, who happened to be visiting the pastor's wife! Without any question, she pulled the crying girl into the house and hugged her to calm her down. For the time being, Sian was rescued.

The good that emerged from this frightening incident was that now Mama Ang's close friends suddenly noticed how beautiful and obedient Sian was as a young maiden. She was diligent, intelligent, and, most important for youth, modest and polite to all she met, especially if they were of her mother's age or older. What an eligible girl blossoming into adulthood! Surely, she was ready for marriage. She could take care of her husband, her children, her home, her parents-in-law, and, of course, her own beloved mother even better. Honoring one's elders was a strong point in traditional Chinese culture, just like in ancient biblical statutes. (Could it be that one of those wise men from the East was a Chinese e.g. the color red is a Chinese symbol for prosperity while red also represents God's ultimate blessing to mankind because Christ poured out His blood for many for the forgiveness of sin? Time will tell.)

It so happened at that juncture that a young man called Ah Li appeared from China.

Chapter 3

Ah Li

China 1910

Born in 1910 in his Hokkien village of *Ch'ng Tau* in *Fujian Province*, a two-hour car ride from *Amoy* (modern *Xiamen*), Ah Li led a sad life too, though his sadness was caused by different factors. His father died when he was two and his mother when he was nine. Orphans were customarily by their surviving grandpa, grandma, or their father's oldest living brother in an extended Chinese family community.

However, Ah Li's adoptive uncle was not really kind to him. Therefore, at around age of 14 years, he planned to run away from his village in search of work and education. Being of a lowly background, he had no means to attend school, though he was a boy. Neither could Ah Li's free spirit contain the restrictions of a traditional Chinese village environment. He had to get away to look for his own fortune. His two elder brothers had left for Malaya, but he did not know exactly where they were nor did he have the means to buy a one-way ticket to travel by sea down south. Hence, he schemed and waited.

One late morning, while his uncle was out in the fields working on his farm, the senior man ordered his agile nephew to bring his lunch for him. He had too much work to walk home and back. They were about one mile from home. How the adrenaline pumped in fourteen-year-old Ah Li's blood as he walked and ran toward their village. Yes, he would go back to the house but he was not going to return to the fields. A few weeks ago, he had ventured out to find the route to town where he could find a job to support himself. The one-hour bus ride had seemed a lifetime to a boy who had never gone beyond his family farm before. Now he was traveling over three hours on foot! He planned to save enough for the long road to freedom! Freedom? What was freedom to a poor teenage orphan who, though wanting to get away from adult restrictions, could think of nothing else but *"How am I going to have my next meal?"*

In a relatively secure rural life, he had had enough to fill his stomach each day. Now, all by himself and without a roof over his head, what is the use of freedom? So Ah Li pondered, so he walked and so he ran with these thoughts swirling in his mind . . .

"Who will give me work? Who will teach me how to read and write?"

Ideas and dreams seemed to fly around his head like a swarm of bees! At least, Ah Li was then free to dream.

Then after what seemed like days, he stopped to look around and finally sighted the roofs of distant houses. Near exhaustion, he pushed on and came across a small shop at the corner of a busy street at the edge of town.

The *towkay* (Hokkien word for boss) appeared kind. Hence, the sweaty, hungry, and tired boy, who was also missing his relatives (nasty though some might be), put on a brave front and asked shyly . . .

"Uncle, do you have work for me? I will do anything for you in exchange for food and shelter!"

Before he could finish, Mr. Tan, the shopkeeper, on seeing his sorry state, welcomed him into the back of his tiny shop where, at the sight of home-cooked steaming hot rice, fried minced pork with oyster sauce, and fresh green *choy sum* (a type of leafy vegetable), his daydreams were pushed aside for the time being. Mrs. Tan had just prepared lunch. He need not explain his predicament. Rural boys looking for jobs in town were a common sight.

"Just eat first, Little Brother," invited Mr. Tan.

"Wow, this uncle is so kind and gentle, not like mine at home! Never met someone like this before; I feel safe!" Ah Li thought as he gobbled up the food before him without embarrassment.

Having been trained for house chores from when he was shorter than a broom's height, he offered to do the dishes and sweep the floor after the meal. Mr. and Mrs. Tan watched askance and nodded their heads at each other. As Mr. Tan heard Ah Li's plight over dinner, the elder sat him down for a chat.

"Young man, why don't you help me run my humble business and I will pay you fairly. Would you like to try it out?" Before he could finish, Ah Li replied, *"Uncle Tan, thank you so much! You don't have to pay me, but please teach me how to read and write in exchange for my humble service. I have to learn to read and write because my uncle at home told his sons to do so. Then they will be successful in the world outside not have to live on a farm their whole life like him! I want to do the same. Could you please help me, Mr. Tan?"*

After a brief discussion, Mr. Tan agreed to take him in on the junior's terms. From then on, clever Ah Li worked hard as a shopkeeper by day and led a student's life by night. His dream was coming true. Through sheer diligence, he eventually did read and write. His calligraphy was beautiful too! An orphan lived on the edge of a knife. One either made it in life or failed. Of course, Ah Li wanted to make it!

Before sleeping, the young man often pondered on why the Tans were so good to him. Maybe they had good parents to bring them up. Then he would weep in silence as he thought of having lost his parents as a child. He could hardly remember his father's face and longed for his mother's smile, comfort, and warm embrace. As the youngest of three boys, Mother had more time for him. She suffered much when widowed, having to depend on the husband's brother to unwillingly provide for them. Her hope was in her sons' success so that they could be free. Then, suddenly, she died. The world seemed to collapse on youngest Ah Li! Who would protect him? Who would love him and call him her own? In the heart of every human being born into this world is a deep need to be owned, to be loved, and to belong.

Soon, Ah Li noticed that the Tans prayed and read the Bible every day before they opened the shop to customers early in the morning before sunrise. The loving couple did the same before they retired to their inner room. One day, they explained to him that Jehovah was God's name. He loved the world so much that He gave His only begotten son, Jesus, to die for all their sins so that whoever believed in Him should not perish (suffer eternal separation from the loving holy God) but would know Him as their eternal Father and live with Him always. Ah Li could not grasp the spiritual realm yet; but he did long to have a father again. If this God of love whom Mr. Tan worshipped was real, one day he would also worship and serve Him. For now though, when in need, he would utter a silent prayer of request to this God to meet his need: he needed to earn a living, to be educated, and to meet up with his brothers in Malaya as soon as possible. Time moved too slowly for a young man.

Three years later, at seventeen years old, he managed to get some news of them.

Ah Peh, the oldest of the three brothers, had left the Chinese shores to seek for his fortune in the south seas four years ago. He finally landed in Kuala Kedah situated at the mouth of the Kedah River in a northern state of British Malaya. Marriage to a pragmatic local Chinese woman, Kim, had given him fulfillment, though they were childless. After they adopted a boy, Ah Kwai, and a girl, Ah Gaik, their lives changed from one of boredom to delight! Children truly brought joy to blessed parents. When reunited through another Chinese immigrant, the two brothers were overjoyed to be together, freed to do what they dreamt of when back in China.

Together, Ah Peh and Kim helped Ah Li get acclimatized to the local culture. The privilege of having an elder caring brother's family at hand has enabled a shy foreigner to overcome the transition from a monocultural Chinese village to a multicultural Malayan urban life. Their nearness brought much healing to his youngest brother's life of loneliness and a sense of lostness. At least, they had one another! Big sister-in-law, Kim, also treated him well. Food was abundant for the fishing family while Ah Li earned some pocket money by working for his brother.

Life was good for a while. Ah Li grew to like the environment in friendly Malaya where Indians, Malays, Chinese, and even *Kwai Loh* (a Cantonese term for white Westerners who were the British of the time) got on quite well. Many of the locals actually spoke Hokkien while the lingua franca in Kuala Kedah (till this day) was colloquial Malay as the majority of the fishermen were Malays. Malaya was his new home. This was where he would marry, have children, and work for his fortune. He felt really good to belong at last! He belonged to his eldest brother and to his new neighbors. He had a potentially good future ahead of him.

However, after about ten months, Ah Li, born with an adventurous spirit, felt restless once more. He wanted to be his own boss. When Ah Peh gave the green light for him to travel south to the town of Taiping (*Great Peace* in Chinese) where most people also spoke Hokkien, his mother tongue, Ah Li set off to look for a job there. With a short list of names and telephone numbers of Ah Peh's friends, he traveled south and eventually reached the pleasant and cooler town of Taiping in the tin-rich state of Perak. Some of the Hokkiens of southern China seemed to have congregated in this town as well.

Meanwhile, Ah Li also wished to find his second Big Brother, Ah Chek. Ah Peh could not stand Ah Chek's fussiness and critical spirit over everything in his household, so they had to part company after a few months in Kedah. The latter was the most educated of the three boys. He could have settled in scenic Penang Island where Sir Francis Light landed and which the British government later developed into a modern educational town peppered with British cuisine, dance, music, and sports. He could also be in Taiping as both towns were Hokkien speaking.

Pleasantly, Ah Li discovered that Taiping was rather different from Kuala Kedah. Here, the air was cooler and fresher. Most of the people were Chinese who had their own small businesses such as the running of coffee shops, restaurants, tailoring shops, vegetables and poultry farms, small rubber estates, market stalls, and food stalls. Having the highest average annual rainfall in Malaya helped the farmers indeed. A smattering of the more educated became teachers, private tutors, and, of course, civil servants in the local government offices.

It was interesting to note that though some Malayan overseas Chinese were into businesses, for example, tin mining, banking, and commerce, others worked long hours to eke a living by becoming strong laborers who fulfilled the necessary manual tasks in town or provided transport in the mode of local *trishaws* (tricycles with attached space in front for passengers).

Many well-trained Chinese women also came from China to serve the richer, more naturalized Chinese as long-term domestic maids. These pigtailed, diligent, and rather perfectionistic ladies came to Malaya with the intention of earning a living as live-in maids. It was a lucrative business then to be an agent to bring them in to serve the elite or not so elite. As long as one can afford to house, feed, and pay them, you may employ one directly or through their association. Most maids were treated well while mutual respect and courtesy was the rule of the day. Many British children were nurtured by these faithful maids from overseas. Even when one wanted to sack an ineffective or dishonest maid, the discharge would be relatively peaceful, fair, and polite. Shakespeare's milk of human kindness seemed to flow more in that era when a deeper sense of community still prevailed. Many local teenagers and married women also work as local maids in middle-class households of various backgrounds. Education for girls was yet to be taken seriously by many Malayan families. Though they might not have been as well trained for humble service, many loyal ones become part of the boss's family members for decades to come. A few had become indispensable and were well rewarded by their generous and kind mistresses who provided for them till death.

As Ah Li's world widened, he noticed that the delightful Indians, mostly brought by the British from India, were mainly either estate and railway workers or senior clerks in government offices. Eventually, some ran restaurants catering spicy Indian cuisines. The Malays main livelihood in this town then was more agricultural, for example, padi (rice) planting and the running of family orchards. Many had roots in the surrounding archipelago in southeast Asia.

Nevertheless, the civil service consisted of staff from a good mix of racial, religious, and cultural backgrounds as long as they worked well and were honest. Existential problems rear their ugly heads anywhere and everywhere on earth. It was just that in those days, life was less hectic when the nation's population was lower and most people were rather contented to have enough to live on day by day. It was fascinating for Ah Li, who came from a relatively monoculture society, to experience living in a peaceful multicultural society!

This was the Malaya that Ah Li landed on in the early twentieth century.

After a few months in Taiping, he discovered that his second brother, Ah Chek, was in Penang which was a two-hour bus ride away. Ah Chek finally had a base in the larger town where he worked as a clerk for a local Chinese firm. However, Ah Li's reunion with his second brother was not as exuberant! Being a rather rigid fellow, Ah Chek made Ah Li feel as if he was disturbing him and as if he was begging for a living from him. Actually, Ah Li was just overjoyed to meet him and thought that he might find a better job in Penang through second brother's contacts. Nevertheless, being an easygoing and flexible person, Ah Li soon overlooked Ah Chek's idiosyncrasies. In between sharing a room with his second brother and job hunting, he walked around the jetty area on the northeastern coast of Penang Island and enjoyed the local nonya hawker food for a few days before taking the shaky old bus to return to Taiping. That was when he learned that at times, good friends might be closer than his own brother. He had a few such friends in Taiping already. One was his new boss, Mr. Ooi.

Mr. Ooi owned a bicycle repair shop by the western end of Taiping town, near to the main road to Penang in the northwest. He provided Ah Li with a camp bed to use in the small shop space by night and work in the same space by day. The meager salary was more than enough for the budget conscious Ah Li to cover his own food and few personal needs. To save even a few cents a month, he might have to take a second night job, if Mr. Ooi allowed. To Ah Li, all nonessentials must wait. Of course, he would like to have better food, clothes, and a bicycle to call his own one day.

Meanwhile, he learnt much about bicycle tyre care and especially about tyre repairs. Ah Li liked to watch the bubbles appear in a basin of water when he immersed the inflated tyre to show the location of a puncture. It felt really good to discover the culprit, which was usually a rusty nail. Since most people used the bicycle for daily transportation, Mr. Ooi's business bloomed! He never allowed his workers to short change his customers. He treated them fairly and expected a high standard repair job from them. Satisfied customers made a happy boss who, in turn, made contented workers!

But once a while, Ah Li envied a rich man's son who was about his age. His driver often dropped him at the air-conditioned restaurant next door to their bicycle shop. He envied how he dressed well, drove a smashing imported British car, and often treated his girlfriends to the one and only cinema in the old Taiping town!

"No worries," mused Ah Li at times, *"one day, I will be having that type of life . . . I just have to be patient and wait for a good wife to help me run a big business!"*

Chapter 4

The Moment of Faith

Taiping 1931

From the time Ah Hoo Ma and the pastor's wife sheltered and protected Sian from Ah Huat, the spoilt rich kid, Mama Ang trusted them. She often wondered why these new friends cared for them so much. Why should they be bothered with a poor mother and her daughter, carrying the stigma of having separated from their husband and father, respectively? She did not have to wait long for the answer.

One day in April, the washerwoman invited Mrs. Lim, the pastor's wife, for a simple dinner at home. Saw wanted to find out more about her life. After the initial *standing-on-ceremony* greetings, Mrs. Lim helped her understand that God loves all people in the world. He created us to love us, not to lose us. Soon, illiterate Mama Ang was asking her to teach her how to read so that she too could read the lyrics of hymns. Therefore, Mrs. Lim taught her to read the alphabets by using a Romanized Hokkien song book as a launchpad. Soon, Mama Ang could read enough to sing hymns with her small group of friends.

One day, as she was singing to herself while waiting for her sponge cakes to rise, she felt a deep sense of her own sins, especially that of her anger against her husband Papa Saw and hatred of his mistress. Then, somehow, her anger was gone, and she no longer saw their sins but her own. A heavy burden was lifted from her shoulders, and she cried with inexplicable joy. Mama Ang simply burst out in song to thank Jesus for dying on the cross for her sins against Him and not just fellowmen. Though her circumstances stayed the same, her attitude had been transformed to one of gratefulness for what she had now: her dear and loyal daughter and friends who accepted, understood and helped her start afresh as a single mother. Finally, she had a heavenly Father who would always be with her, be there for her, and would never leave her in a lurch! By faith she would live from now onwards, freed from the shackles of jealousy, shame, confusion, and rejection. But how did her one and only daughter, Sian, respond to her mother's life transformation?

Young Sian was terribly angry and confused that her mother had stopped worshipping the deities in their home, especially that of the goddess of mercy, to whom she had been dedicated. Furthermore, since they received news that Papa Saw had died, according to the traditional Chinese practice of ancestral honor, she was the one who daily placed joss sticks at and bowed to an ancestral tablet each morning to remember Papa Saw, no matter how he had hurt her dear Mama. However, Christians believed that they should bow down to worship Jesus only. So how could she change her god? If she too followed her Mama to worship Jesus, who would worship the deities and honor Papa Saw? Only she was available to carry on this duty if Mother refused to do it now as Christians believed their God is the one and only true and living God. No, she could not become a Christian. However, she was smart enough to yearn to read and write. At least, she must be able to read for herself to find out what was going on in the world around her!

After her Mama's sudden spiritual experience shocked her, Sian pleaded with Mrs. Lim to tutor her as well. Her urge to be literate soon overshadowed her anxiety over the ancestral worship matter. She was growing older by the day. It would be wiser to be able to read and write before she had a family when child rearing and housework would take most of her time and energy. Therefore, the pastor's wife became the familiar tutor in their small room once more. This time round, since Mama Ang's hymn singing had familiarized Sian with the lyrics, Mrs. Lim used the Romanized Hokkien Bible as the launchpad instead.

Week after week, they plodded through that timeless book. By the time they reached the end of the book called Matthew, the first book in the New Testament part of the Bible, Sian voluntarily wanted to be baptized! She had had her eyes of faith opened to see that Jesus truly is the Son of God who had freely given Himself to all mankind. Since this God did not reject her but welcomed her to be His disciple, He is indeed worthy of her whole life. Yes, if she had to confess her sins to Him and ask Him to take over her life, she would. One can only imagine the joy in the heart of one totally forgiven of all her sins against the God of truth and grace. Mother and daughter were not only reconciled with God their Father and Jesus their Savior, they were also truly reconciled with each other deep down inside. Home would never be the same again. They saw themselves as God's beloved daughters, dignified and fulfilled, poor though they were on earth. They saw themselves as pilgrims on the way to Him, not refugees running away to another country due to their family problems. Furthermore, they had learnt that all God's children were equal in His eyes, whether they were rich or poor, literate or illiterate, male or female, young or old and healthy or sick.

"No wonder," Sian pondered, *"no wonder Ah Hoo Ma and Mrs. Lim could love us like their own family!"*

Though they could not grasp truth in scholarly theological terms, they could grasp truth in their hearts and minds in their personalized unique ways as long as they were guided by the Bible given to them. What purpose, what joy filled their lives from then on!

Consequently, when Ah Li asked Ah Hoo Ma (who often had her punctured bicycle tyres repaired at his shop) to matchmake Sian with him, the senior friend explained to him the Good News of Jesus being our Savior before doing so. After a few weeks, on his own accord (for he was a strong willed young man who could not be forced to change his mind about anything), he was convinced of the reality that Jesus is the Truth, the Way and the Life and eventually asked for baptism in obedience to Jesus, the Savior. Ah Li reassured Ah Hoo Ma that he did not do this just to marry Sian; he did this because he had met Jesus and believed His word. If he did not have the same faith in Christ, he would not marry Sian, even though he would feel very sad. He understood that two could not live together happily if they did not agree on this very important issue of faith in God from whom come life, truth and grace.

Chapter 5

Marriage and Motherhood

Taiping 1932

Time and again, over the last few months, when Ah Hoo Ma dropped by the roadside shop to repair her bicycle, the boss had praised his worker, Ah Li, before her. The former had also watched how honest and diligent Ah Li was at the tyre repair shop down the road. There was once, when she overpaid Ah Li for the job done, he promptly returned the excess to her. Therefore, when Ah Li requested Ah Hoo Ma to be his matchmaker, she was not surprised.

One fine Saturday, Ah Hoo Ma brought a red packet enclosing a gift of money to Mama Ang as a way of expressing Ah Li's formal proposal to her beautiful daughter, Sian. Mama Ang was simply overjoyed! At last, if she should not be around, Sian would have a responsible husband to care for her. She would be in safe hands. Mama Ang had one condition i.e. Ah Li must promise to provide Sian with proper transport if Sian's damaged hip hurt one day. In response, Ah Li assured her of his loving tender care for Sian for the rest of their life together. He would also try his best to buy a car for Sian as soon as he had earned enough. However, as was the Chinese custom then, the engaged couple could only meet each other at the girl's home. The shy couple sat in the little front room to communicate in the presence of Mama Ang. If he were to date her outside her home, an older female chaperon would be necessary. On hindsight, this cautious practice seemed wiser than today's free-for-all relationships causing a deep and wide social dilemma, though the guidelines for dating could have been slightly more flexible.

Once the wedding date was announced, the whole church community rejoiced with the migrant mother and daughter and the well liked Ah Li! They saw this as God's reward for humble Ah Li and Sian! Together, they would go far in life and be a blessing to others!

Therefore, fellow church members took it upon themselves to give them the grandest yet modest feast they could. Everyone was involved: some planned the menu and cooked whereas others worked out a most blessed church wedding service for them. Friends who knew them through daily contacts also chipped in. Ah Li's eldest brother and sister-in-law, Kim, and their children also travelled from Kedah to rejoice with them. They were very happy that Ah Li finally had a wife to care of him too. He was now an independent young man with a wife to walk with him and an understanding mother-in-law to spoil him! What a blessing for a poor orphan from an unknown village in China. He would be *orphaned* no more!

Secretly, Ah Li, the excited bridegroom, vowed to God and to himself that he would treasure and care for Sian and her mother as his new and precious family.

Time did tell that Ah Li's promises were real in his own ways. He took great care of his considerate mother-in-law and mutually submissive Sian. He was determined to earn enough to provide for his family. His kind, generous, firm, and humble ways were admired by friends and relatives alike. It was, therefore, not surprising that Sian's friends quickly approved of him.

A few months after the wedding, Sian conceived, and their first child was born in early 1933. Mama Ang's household members had doubled instantly! The chubby infant had the cutest round cheeks like Sian and rough dark hair like Ah Li. They named her Mei Li. This time round, both parents did not really have any gender preference for their first born, though Chinese culture would have dictated that a son was preferred. Sian's deprivation of literacy had opened their eyes to cultural favoritism, though prejudice die hard indeed.

How their lives were changed. Now Ah Li worked faster at the shop so that he could be home to be with Sian to relieve her by bathing Mei Li so that Sian could prepare dinner. Mama Ang (now promoted to being called Grandma Ang), meanwhile, continued to earn some extra cash with her small laundry and baking business.

So Mei Li grew in size, in laughter and in cheekiness. Soon, she grew in her hymn singing to the God of her parents and her God. What a happy family living in simplicity and childlike faith a day at a time! Oh yes, they would love to have more babies if they could!

When she turned three, her parents felt it was time to move on from Taiping. They had some savings to use during the transition period. Ah Li had learnt a trade in dealing with bicycle parts and repairs. One day, he would import and export them, not just repair old bicycle tyres. Where should they settle down for the long term? Thoughts of being nearer one of his brothers came to mind. To shift to Kuala Kedah where Ah Peh lived would be great. However, he had no inclination for fishing or the sale of fish products. Furthermore, he felt that the river mouth village would be too hot for his family. Then his thoughts turned to Ah Chek, his other brother. In spite of the latter's sternness and seeming unfriendliness, a brother was still a brother. After months of discussion with Sian and Mama

Ang, they finally decided for Penang Island as their new home. Georgetown, the capital of Penang state, lay on its northeastern coastline where a cross channel ferry shuttled passengers to and fro between the island and mainland.

When they shared this news with their good friends, Pastor Lim was roped in to introduce them to members of a Chinese church in Georgetown. They would ensure a smooth adaption to Penang Island life.

"Islanders tend to have a unique island mentality which mainland dwellers do not understand," explained Ah Hoo Ma.

"I will make sure you have church members to help you find a house to rent and a job to start with. Their church will be a second home to you. God's children are in His one huge family. Soon Mei Li will need to attend school. Not to worry, everything will be taken care of. My relatives there can also help you. Just give me a few weeks to arrange the details with them."

When Ah Li heard these encouraging words, he silently thanked God in his heart. Tonight, when he prayed with the family, they would give thanks to Him together.

Chapter 6

The Penang Adventure

Penang 1936

True enough, when the family of four reached Penang Island by a borrowed car for their few simple belongings, they drove straight to the house of Pastor Hsu. Mrs. Hsu warmly welcomed the tired family warmly with an attractively prepared home-cooked lunch! Immediately, they felt at home in the parsonage and knew that they were genuinely accepted as members of the larger family of God. They stayed in their guest rooms till a cheap two-bedroom upstairs unit in Love Lane was available for rental. The next step was to look for a job for survival. Looking up the newspapers for jobs was wise but, even in those days, recommendation by friends worked faster.

Ah Chong, a friend of Pastor Hsu, owned a bicycle import and export shop a few streets from their new address. Through some negotiations, Ah Li was soon employed to be his assistant. With his experience with bicycles, his being a Hokkien, and his self-taught Mandarin, Ah Li was called to work immediately. Overjoyed, he ran home to Sian to announce this great news!

"Kam-Sia Chu (Thanks be to God)! Wah oo kang-liow (I have a job now)!" he shouted excitedly as he jumped up the narrow stairs of their tiny home.

"In fact, I can learn how to do big business from this shop! The boss actually buys bicycles from overseas and sells them here!" he added.

"Let's have a feast tonight, Sian! You have enough fresh chicken? I'll do the cooking!"

Through his need to survive on his own, Ah Li had become quite a chef in his own right. He could whip up a scrumptious meal in no time when his Taiping boss wanted to entertain his business guests at home. He would also give him lots of the remnants, which he used to bring home for his family to eat for another one to two meals. Those were also the days when he developed a taste for good food . . . yum!

In this joyful atmosphere, Sian conceived again.

When Mei Li turned four, Mei Ren, their second daughter arrived. She was safely delivered at home by a local traditional midwife. She probably had much more experience for normal deliveries than a British-trained one at the Penang General Hospital. It was too complicated to attend the latter as they did not understand or speak English. However, a small cloud hovered over this blessed family for a while . . .

Ah Li had hoped for a son. Though he loved the little infant in his arms, it took him some time to accept the fact that until then, he still had no heir to his surname, Teh.

You see, most men could live with their thinking cap and emotions apart most of the time. Their brains seem to be wired that way. They could think right but feel wrong or vice versa. They also usually communicated with their minds instead of with their feelings at a deeper level of consciousness. At times, a couple could be torn apart because the man was just unable to have heart-to-heart talks with his wife. On the other hand, the woman yearned for more intimacy and for more of a sense of feeling that she was heard and understood by the man to whom she has given her body and soul. She did not really want him to follow everything she wanted.

When the first child was a girl, the novelty of having a child of his own so overwhelmed Ah Li that he soon forgot about preferring a boy. There was always hope that the next child would be a son for his own fulfillment. However, if the second child was also a girl, his disappointment cut deeper and stayed longer. So Ah Li struggled with his ability to accept Mei Ren for who she was. In many ways, she was perfect, intelligent, and fast but . . . she was a girl! To hide his mental and emotional torment, Ah Li worked even harder in order to save for a better lifestyle. At least, money in hand was a tangible comfort. But as the months flew by and Mei Ren grew up to become a fine and obedient three-year-old daughter, Papa Ah Li's heart melted and his feelings for her normalized. He was proud to be her Papa as well.

Meanwhile, wonderfully upbeat Mama Ang took up a new home-based trade to supplement their household income. That was how loving extended families cared for one another. She sewed fashionable western-type dresses and Chinese sam-fu for the neighbors' children and women. Word passed round that there was a skilled tailor in the vicinity. Within a year, Mama Ang had more orders than she could cope with each day. Hence, in between mothering, cooking, cleaning, and washing, Sian watched her beloved mother working and picked up the trade as well. By the time Mei Li reached seven and Mei Ren, four, they too helped pick up or cut threads or unpick simple stitches when something was wrongly sewn. They did not have a sewing machine yet; so hand-sewn stitches were rather large and easy to undo. Ah Li liked watching them in action and promised himself that one day, he would buy a strong and lasting *Singer* sewing machine for the ladies!

By and by, a weekly routine developed in the home.

Come Saturday nights, young and old slept by 10:00 p.m. in order to get up fresh the next morning for worship times at their Chinese church. *Sundays* were off work days for Ah Li's family. The local Methodist church members had become their second family and the venue, their second home. They felt comfortable there as the rich and the poor sat together to worship God and to feed on the Word of God taught from the pulpit. When it came to giving for God's work, a trishaw puller was at much at ease as a rich chauffeured *towkay*, even if the former could give much less offering each week. Did not Jesus affirm and praise the widow who put in two cents into an offering box because she had given all that she had? It was the sacrificial God honoring heart that counted in the heavenly Father's eyes. Who could out-give the Creator of the heavens and the earth, any way.

Sunday afternoons were well spent unwinding at the Penang Botanical Gardens (a twenty-minute bus ride away), at the Tanjong Bungah beach front (a thirty-minute bus trip away) where all learnt to swim, even Mama Ang, or at the foothills of Penang Hill in the Air Itam wet market (a fifteen-minute bus trip away). At the last named, there was a variety of cheap and delicious local Penang hawker food! Till today, locals and foreign tourists would rush to queue for a table at the famous roadside *assam laksa* (a Malay Thai fishmint and prawn paste soup noodle dish) stall!

"*Maybe,*" mused Sian to herself one Sunday, "*if Ah Li's dream of owning a bicycle shop is not fulfilled, I could open such a stall. Meanwhile, just enjoy it-lah!*"

Then, suddenly, she came back to the present as she heard a crash of crockery behind her. She turned and just saw Ah Li leaping off his seat and hopping on one foot as the waitress accidentally dropped a bowl of that delicious hot soup just behind his back. If not for the seriousness of the situation, she would have laughed aloud at his stance! But manners must prevail, especially for a smart looking lady like her.

Next on the weekly schedule was a *Wednesday* evening 8:00 p.m. after dinner Bible Reading and Prayer Time among all family members and whoever happened to drop by. If visitors do not wish to join in, they were gently requested to wait for a few minutes with a cup of hot tea in their hands. Papa Ah Li would start off with the reading of a short Bible passage from his Chinese Bible, followed by an interpretation-cum-application of the text; then they sang a hymn of that week's needs and another of praise and thanksgiving. For example, if they were stressed up by a current problem, they would sing *I Need Thee Every Hour*; if they were full of joy that a customer had finally paid up his debt to them, then they would sing *Count Your Blessings*. This would be followed by the *memorizing* of a new scripture verse. Since their Savior Jesus used Scriptures to answer Satan, the fallen angel and tempter, they must do the same at the appropriate time, by using His word stored in their memories beforehand. This devout activity would then be closed by short prayers from anyone present. What peace, what restfulness in God every week and each day.

In addition, Ah Li and Sian would pray separately every day: on waking up and before they rested their tired bodies and minds.

During his day off, Ah Li also rediscovered his musical talent of playing on his precious China-made harmonica. As the music filled the air, Mei Li and Mei Ren would automatically and naturally tap their feet and then break into a self-choreographed dance all over the floor of their ten by ten feet big kitchen-cum-dining room-cum-lounge!

One day, they invited Uncle Ah Chek for dinner on a Friday night. The girls were excited as he was the only uncle near enough for them. They helped lay the table and chairs; they were so proud of their mother's cooking and their happy home. Then Uncle arrived on his bicycle. Both girls ran down and hopped out to welcome him up the stairs. They held his hand lovingly, one on each side, but he shook them off and dusted his pure white sleeves. Shocked and not knowing what to do, they felt rejected and stayed away from him ever since. Meanwhile, they decided to watch his behavior from afar. Horror of horrors, he took out a pure white large handkerchief to wipe their shining waxed stool specially cleaned for the guest of honor for the night.

"How could he do that! He is so rude!" whispered the younger to the older girl.

"Shhhhh . . ." cautioned the older, *"Don't let him hear us; let us wait to see what else he will do."*

The sisters' hope of having a friendly uncle around was dashed. Uncle Ah Chek was definitely awkward and stern. He also disliked kids, and they feared him. His phobia of dirt completely turned them off! Grandma Ang had always taught them to give and take. They could not always have their own way. But this uncle not only wore only white shirts and pants, but he also always had a white handkerchief to cover any seat he used, including his old bicycle seat! As they grew older, they discovered that he preferred to live on his own in a rented room without making any friends long enough to become good friends. Who would want to be near him any way.

"See how he treats our Papa," Mei Li shared with Mei Ren that night.

"Uncle expects Papa to show total gratitude to him as a younger brother because this second brother had a part in asking friends to help the youngest one get out of China. But see how our friends love us," they pondered in their childlike minds, *"yet they never ask us to return them anything!"*

So they pondered and felt angry and somewhat confused at such adult misbehavior. But those were rare moments of reflection. Most times the two sisters played and were contented kids in a world of their own!

Soon, as the family united to save what they could, they had more than they needed. Ah Li began to plan to be his own boss. Finally, a neighbor arranged for him to lease a two-storey shophouse in downtown Bishop Street, Georgetown. The ground floor would be used for business and storage of goods while the upstairs would be their living quarters, all in one. They now had more space for the family and for their new venture. Ah Li was rather unaware that running one's own business could cause much headache as well. But then he could save some money from being nearer home. He could also pop upstairs for lunch at any time. Of course, if he wanted to grow his wealth, he had to save some more to expand his business. So Ah Li day-dreamed and smiled to himself. For now, Ah Li felt really affirmed when his former boss wished him well and promised to buy his Japanese bicycles from him one day. A gracious boss would be happy that his worker had outgrown him in business and in life.

Then, in 1940, God gave Ah Li and Sian a son!

Wow, the whole of Bishop Street seemed to rejoice with them! Half the population in that area were Chinese and half were Indians, but all Asians of those days understood the pride in a family when the first son arrived! They had no ultrasound to check on the baby's gender then, but an experienced doctor often guessed right. Actually, his secret was that if the fetus were a male, the pregnant mother had more body hair, especially in the pubic area, simply because she had more male hormones (known as androgens) floating in her blood! A more knowledgeable doctor would have a better chance of prediction and would be lauded as an excellent doctor if he guessed right.

If not, it would be taken as only a joke! Doctors were loved by their trusting patients for their compassion, not their prophetic ability.

So firecrackers could be heard all around Bishop Street, China Street, Church Street and Penang Street when Mama Ang (the oldest in a traditional Chinese family must be mentioned first as a sign of respect), Ah Li, Sian, Mei Li, and Mei Ren celebrated Ah Keat's full moon day (i.e. when thirty days old) according to the Chinese lunar calendar. Friends brought gifts while the family entertained them with red-dyed eggs, red oval Chinese cakes filled with lotus paste and the famous *nonya* curry chicken (it had to be as they were now Penangites, not just traditional Chinese.) Penang had a natural blend of traditional Malay and Chinese cultures reflected in their daily food, clothing, conversation and mannerisms. In fact, Mei Li grew up not knowing that some of the words local residents used had their roots in the Malay vocabulary (e.g., the Malay word for 'stone' is *batu*. But Penang children thought it was a Chinese word for 'stone').

Hence, though Ah Li spoke with a strong mainland China accent, Sian and the children spoke with the distinctive Penang slang. However, many second-generation Chinese migrant children had integrated so well into the local cultures that they could switch between the Chinese, English, and Malay lingua if they were speaking to those who came from the different language groups at the same time. Later in the twentieth century, Ah Li and Sian's descendants realized that they were so privileged to have been there at that time, as Malaysians, as a trial run to the future inevitable twenty-first century globalized multicultural, multiracial and multireligious world community! It mattered not where they lived. Societies in many countries have become similar in population variety! Crossing cultures has become a necessary universal phenomenon. Could this be a preparation to live in a future dimension where every tribe, tongue, and nation would be represented?

Back home in Bishop Street, Penang, Ah Li's and Sian's family atmosphere became more jovial after Ah Keat arrived as Papa Ah Li, the head of the family, now felt fulfilled with his heir in tow . . . the Chinese way.

Chapter 7

War in Nation, War at Home

Malaya 1942–1945

Japan declared war on South-East Asia. World War II finally reached Malaya on December 8, 1941. On the Kelantan beach, the hard and stern looking patriotic soldiers, loyal only to their general, landed stealthily into a relatively leisurely British Malaya. Kelantan state was northeast of Penang state.

Ah Li's newly leased shophouse was right in town near to where the British had its fort at the Esplanade which faced east. Fort Cornwallis, their stronghold, stood by the sea and was just a mere ten minutes' walk away. When the evening air cooled down, Ah Li and his workers would sometimes take the kids for a slow stroll to the jetty up the road or to the Esplanade adjacent to the fort. At the jetty, travelers, who daily travel both ways between the island and mainland of Penang, caught the cross channel ferries to work and home. The children loved to watch the huge ferries arriving and leaving with tired passengers rushing down from the upper level to get home as soon as they could. These same ferries also took them to Prai, an otherwise small town by the sea opposite to this part of the island, to catch the Malaya Railways train north to Thailand or south to

Singapore. Papa Li's workers adored the kids and often treated them with candies or ice balls sold by the roadside.

Then, suddenly, the serenity of Penangites was broken by the sound of bombs all around them. Bishop Street lay adjacent to the busy commercial banking area where enemies might target. After consultation with neighbors, friends, and church members, Sian's family decided to find shelter in the foothills of Penang Hill. Throughout the war, they lived in the fresh greenery of a Chinese village hidden in Paya Terubong at the foothills of Penang Hill (currently renamed Bukit Bendera, i.e., Flag Hill).

Wars caused hardship to ordinary citizens who were usually not involved in the political struggles of the day. This war was not different from others. Many families with young, old, and weak members suffered much loss and grief when a loved one is tortured and/or killed. Poverty ensued if the man in the house was gone. Thankfully, neighborly care for one another prevailed in a less individualistic age. Ah Mm, an elderly grandmother, who worked together with her son in the making of granite tombstones in the hills, had a tender spot for Sian's family. She got along well with Mama Ang and helped her family with supplies from her vegetable garden, fruit orchard, and chicken and duck coops. If on their own, sometimes they had no other vegetables but potato or yam leaves. These were delicious and spicy when fried with *sambal belachan* (a Malay recipe of pound chilly mixed with prawn paste and salt). Furthermore, whenever Ah Mm thumped a bicycle ride to the nearby wet market, she would return with gifts for her grandchildren as well as for Mei Li, Mei Ren, and Ah Keat. It was so nurturing and safe for the children to have two grandmothers—a medium sized natural Grandma Ang and a buxom special Grandma Ah Mm to give them huge warm hugs as they squealed with laughter ever so often. Oblivious to the harshness of war, children cope well. To them, ignorance is bliss! During the day, both grandmothers kept an eye on them as well as led them by the hand over rough patches of earthy "playgrounds" in the hills. They loved the sound of the clear rippling stream behind their temporary wooden hut. Temporary? How long was the war going to last? When could they visit their townhouse again? Had thieves broken in to cart away their livelihood? After waiting for three weeks, Ah Li could not stand it any longer.

Early one morning, when the bombing had stopped for a few days, and after prayers for protection with Mama Ang, Sian, and the children, he cycled as fast as he could, avoiding enemy soldiers here and there to finally reach his shop.

"Heavenly Father," he prayed before entering by the backdoor, *"please let everything be as I left them. The new bicycle parts purchased on credit and the tyres stacked in the corner at the back near the toilet. I need to come back to earn for my family when war is over. Please, Father, I plead."*

God heard him. Everything was in order, though business could not proceed at the moment. With a quick thanksgiving,

"Kam sia Chu!" (*"Thank God"* in Hokkien).

Then he washed up, changed, and prepared for the return trip. Before leaving, Ah Li placed his ear on the wall and strained his ears for sounds from their neighbors. Silence prevailed.

"I wonder how they are," he uttered to himself. *"I pray that they were not killed like our church friend's husband and his mistress."*

This couple had hidden themselves under the bed when the siren howled; both were killed by a bomb, which happened to land right on top of their hiding place. It might be easy to hide from one's wife but not from a bomb.

When he heard an army truck in the distance, Ah Li hastily stuffed his pockets with dollar bills sewn into a pillow, picked up what Sian and Mama Ang had ordered, hid the valuables in more secure secret nooks and corners, and then made the journey back. If he paddled hard, he might make it home in forty-five minutes.

What shouts of relief when Mei Ren saw him coming up the country path to their hut.

"Papa is home! Papa is home!" she yelled and added, *"The soldiers didn't catch him!"*

Soon everyone in the neighborhood was crowding around Ah Li to catch some updated news of the deserted town. Yes, it was quite safe and easy to avoid the soldiers. There were not many around. Several houses had their roofs blown off while some were burnt beyond recognition though the jetty area remained intact. Maybe the Japanese needed the jetty and railways for transport too and avoided those places. Finally, the VIP was able to unload his goodies for the family. He was also able to refund some money to Ah Mm who had been so kind to them. She treated them as part of her family and never complained of the row they made at meal times.

Soon Sian had a fourth strong baby girl, Mei En. Mama Ang nee Grandma Ang became her main babysitter except for feeding times as Sian did the harder work of chopping firewood for cooking and doing other house chores. The two big sisters and one big brother loved to take turns to play with Mei En every day and any time they could. Learning to read and practicing writing and arithmetic at home could become boring after a while. This was the first time they lived in the rural area and they just loved the space and variety of plants and flowers growing wild. They would make full use of nature before they shifted home. In fact, Ah Keat preferred to stay there forever as the active boy could jump, kick, and fish safely and freely, with two sisters to watch over him. With more space to move around, he bumped into his siblings less often and hardly broke any glass or bowl. Hence, the family cane had a rest as well.

However, one Saturday, tragedy struck this friendly village community. A neighbor's five year old son, Boy-Boy, found a coconut on the ground. He picked it up to bring it to his mother two doors away. As he passed by Ah Li's hut, Grandma Ang was sitting outside with toddler Mei En beside her. Suddenly, Mei En saw a butterfly flirting around her head and decided to catch it. She rushed away from Grandma right into the path of Boy-Boy who was lugging his precious heavy coconut. He fell and the coconut landed on Mei En's head! Her loud scream was followed by a deafening silence. Grandma Ang panicked and got up to hold the little girl slumped just five feet away. Mei En's eyes were closed; she did not respond to Grandma's call or touch. There was no obvious cut on her head. Grandma gently carried her and placed her on her bed. There was no nearby clinic and Sian, Ah Li and the two girls were out for a short while. Grandma put her to bed to rest. As Mei En seemed to sleep peacefully during dinner time, no one wanted to disturb her. The fright of the knock and fall must have tired her out.

However, that night, Mei En developed a high fever but in war time, a nightly curfew prevented them from looking for a doctor. So first thing in the morning, Ah Li took Sian with Mei En in her arms to the downhill clinic. They were worried that she was sleeping so long. By the time the doctor was able to check her, Mei En just breathed her last. How Sian cried and wailed as Ah Li controlled himself and comforted her. When they reached home with the bad news, everyone at home cried uncontrollably. The children would miss their darling sister a lot. They could not understand why God took her away. For days, weeks, and months, they talked about their dearest baby Mei En till they felt consoled. Yes, heavenly Father would take full care of her now. She would grow up in heaven and they would all be so happy to meet her again one day. To those who believe in the God of eternity, dying is like changing one's address though the living grieved. So they comforted one another, and so they were healed of their grief.

Every night, Ah Li held Sian in his arms. On one such night, Ah Li lovingly whispered into Sian's ears,

"If God can give, God can take away, Sian. Everyone and everything belong to Him. We don't understand his purpose yet, but we can trust Him to be good and fair, strong and loving. Let us thank Him for letting us take care of Mei En for eighteen months. We will ask Him for another child . . ."

True enough, two months later, Sian conceived their fifth child! Like a rhythm of sorrow and joy, the household rejoiced and waited with expectancy for baby to arrive. However, due to much physical work, Sian had severe bleeding from the womb and had a miscarriage at twelve weeks gestation. Once more she grieved, once more she endured. Yes, she must take care of her living children and not allow herself to fall into depression (called *sadness or sleep illness* in those days). The words from an old proverb Papa Saw used to repeat to himself came to mind:

"The greatness of a man lies not in never falling but that each time he falls, he gets up again. I wonder where it comes from," she said to herself as she cooked the evening meal a few days later and uttered beneath her heavy sigh (not an academic, Sian took the meaning of *fall* as *suffering* instead of *failure*).

"Heavenly Father, You alone know how I feel . . . please comfort me, I pray."

With that, determined Sian focused all her energy on taking care of the living at home. She would help Ah Li start the new small kerosene lamp factory he mentioned the other day. If the war was going to drag on and on, they had better find other ways of feeding the family. Yes, they could start a new business while Mama Ang was still healthy enough to keep an eye on the children. Furthermore, since electricity was regularly cut off during long hours of nightly curfews, Penangites needed the alternative and cheap energy provided by kerosene lamps. They had better hurry! Once Ah Li was encouraged by his dear wife on anything, he had the confidence to proceed. Two were indeed better than one!

Hence, their low mood at home was miraculously lifted! Daily, they cycled around to friends and acquaintances to work on the start up for their new business. They looked to their good big sister friend, Ah Hoo Ma, for advice and got more than what they dared to ask for. She would share their need with her daughter's father-in-law who lived in Penang. Maybe he could help. True enough, Mr. Chai immediately lent them enough money to start buying the raw materials (e.g. aluminum sheets, wicks, tools, wire and nails) needed to make simple kerosene lamps for domestic uses. A small shop was also rented in the Thean Teik Estate, a ten minute bicycle ride away, on the way to town. It could also double up as a shop front for easy access to customers who walk or ride by.

Ah Li, Sian's partner in charge of business finance, checked out the credit given by the various retail shops before ordering them. Both promised each other to use the money entrusted to them wisely. They would also spend within their means and not incur unnecessary debts.

Mr. Chai, their gentleman creditor, very kindly often acted as a bouncing board for their new business ideas. As he listened to the younger man, he nodded . . . and nodded . . . and nodded with a bemusing smile on his caring face. He told Ah Li much later that, a few months after knowing Ah Li and Sian, he commented to Mrs. Chai, his wife,

"This young couple can be trusted. They've got their heads on their shoulders, they love their family, and they love God. I will turn their loan into a Christmas gift to the family!"

Consequently, Sian enjoyed the double roles of being a wife and a business partner with Ah Li!

Ah Li also felt good except for one matter. He had a niggling thought that if his only son should be killed in war, it would be very hard on him. War was terrible. Anyone might be killed at any time. Now and then the men in the neighborhood received some news of current world and local affairs through the underground Malayan resistance. The Japanese might not leave so soon. If they should, for any reason, lose Ah Keat, he would not have an heir again. For a China born traditional Chinese, it was a critical risk. He thought about this possibility and yearned for another son. The devil began to play on his mind.

One afternoon, after seeing to his errands in town, he visited an older business friend, Lai, on the way home from his shophouse. As they chatted and shared about their families, Lai suggested that he took a mistress to give him another son. Anyway, Ah Li needed to relax more. Another woman in his life would not harm him or his family. He could pay for her and did not have to steal someone else's woman. At first, being a good family man and a Christian, Ah Li rejected the idea totally. He loved Sian dearly and would not think of hurting her a bit. However, like dripping water on the head, Lai's persuasion made headway when Ah Li went for his usual haircut in town, near to the shophouse.

Chin Chin, his new hairdresser (in war time, hairdressers doubled up as barbers even when unisex saloons were unknown), looked more charming than usual that Monday. Her body language attracted Ah Li, and soon a friendship was formed. She was the only other woman he had talked with at close proximity, and he felt good around her.

Chin Chin lived with her mother. One day, the latter left for Ipoh to visit her son's family. As it happened, Ah Li dropped by for another haircut soon after the previous one. As he lingered on till business closed for the day, Chin Chin indicated her fear of being on her own for the first time since war started.

Japanese soldiers could do much harm to single ladies. As she was speaking, thoughts ran through Ah Li's mind:

"I never had a sister before. I treat her like my own sister. It won't harm her or me if I stay one night in her shop to keep her company. She is all alone. She can sleep in her own room and I in mine. It will be for only one night."

Careless with his own weaknesses, Ah Li did just that without questioning his own reasoning. He fell head over heels into Chin Chin's web and she became his secret mistress.

At home, Ah Li began to change his behavior. He started to lie about having to stay overnight in town. He had to guard their shophouse from thieves. An unconfessed lie inevitably led to another lie in order to cover up the previous one. Eventually, Sian sensed something wrong in him. He was not as keen to have sex with her over a few weeks. This caused Sian to cycle to town on her own to personally see for herself where he was. Ah Li was not at the shophouse. When she asked around the neighborhood, one kind lady informed her that he was seeing a hairdresser who lived in the next street. Sian's trusting heart sank. When confronted at home, Ah Li vehemently denied the affair and accused the neighbor of breaking up his family. Ah Li appeared more subdued but continued his secret affair.

Then, as time passed by, Ah Li stayed away overnight again, with the excuse that he had late dinners with men friends. It was dangerous for him to cycle home under the influence of alcohol. On one such nights, Sian felt that she had to check on him once more.

Suddenly, into the anxious and sensitive family landed an even more drastic emotionally charged war! The difference between this war at home and that war in the nation was that this war was definitely preventable. Thus began a long journey of sorrow in a once happy home; a long journey of disloyalty, jealousy, strife, wastage of funds and broken hearts in Sian and their children.

In 1944, Sian was only thirty-one and blessed with beautiful sharp features and an ivory smooth complexion. She was capable, able to multitask, and was physically strong enough to cycle anywhere alone or with others. She loved life and her fear of God and her faith in Him kept her loyal to family and friends. She had a modest and humble attitude and was generous yet discerning and firm in making decisions. Though illiterate (not by choice), no one could cheat her in her dealings with creditors and debtors alike. How did such a good woman respond to her husband's infidelity when the cat came out of the bag?

Sian fought back in intense anger. It was just not right! She had slogged with her one and only man for years for the security of their children! Didn't she sacrifice her time with the children to help start this new business with him? She did not sacrifice her other richer and more handsome suitors to share her husband with another woman! His injustice must be stopped in its path! Since she did not know who the lady was, except that she was a hairdresser from town, she must see for herself what sort of woman she was. She had some loyal lady friends who would spy for her.

True enough, news came to her one September noon that Ah Li would be taking Chin Chin to the Odeon cinema in Penang Road that evening. Sian left her children with her Mama Ang and cycled as fast as she could to reach the cinema hall in thirty minutes before the show was to start. As soon as she spotted Ah Li meeting Chin Chin at the ticket counter, she walked up to them, caught Chin Chin by her hair, gave her a hard slap on her face, and pushed her away from a shocked Ah Li. Loud angry words and nasty names were then hurled at Chin Chin who had stolen her husband. When Ah Li tried to stop her actions and words, he too was scolded. Women in Asian cultures were brought up to feel guilt and shame more astutely. Thus, Chin Chin disappeared as fast as she appeared. With head bowed, she ordered a trishaw and got away in a split second. That horrifying night, two very broken individuals made their way home to the hills separately. Their children needed them.

How did Ah Li feel?

Humiliated publicly by a woman, the chauvinist Ah Li brewed in his heart, though he controlled himself in public. Afraid that his anger might cause him to harm the family, he calmed himself down before reaching home by taking a longer route to the Paya Terubong hills. The physical exercise did good to his soul. He began to enjoy the fresh night breeze as it fanned his tired face to wash his anger and guilt away. Yes, he had wronged his wife through his foolish relationship with another woman. He would try his best to change his hairdresser. Maybe he shold look harder for a barber instead.

For days, as Sian, in tears, poured out her disappointment with Ah Li to Mama Ang, the peacemaker, the loving Mama comforted her one and only daughter. She helped Sian to see the relationship objectively. Mama knew that though Ah Li had his weakness with women, she was glad to have a diligent son-in-law who respected her, an old lady. Basically, Ah Li was a family man and Mama Ang could see that he loved Sian. He would come to his sense; she was sure of that happening.

As a result, after what seemed like years of cold war for a once loving and united family, though it was only a week, Sian told Ah Li she had forgiven him but warned him not to betray her again. Their pastor and his wife visited to pray for them and supported this emotionally fragile sister and brother in God's family. Their doors were always open for those in need. Ah Hoo Ma, the matchmaker, was also summoned to arbitrate. She tried her best to persuade Ah Li to change his ways and not repeat his mistake.

Feeling insecure now that her husband seemed to be repeating her own father's mistake, Sian began to save from that day onwards. She had seen how difficult it was for Mama Ang to bring her up. No, this must not happen to her children, especially when she could not earn much if left in a lurch. Her illiteracy did not help. But she would save as much money as she could from now. And so she did.

For a while, Ah Li spent time more time with Sian to reassure her of his loyalty. But soon, Sian knew he was lying about the other woman again. Should she spy on him to stop him once more? Should she be wiser to pretend ignorance, which would be peace at home?

Just at this juncture of their family life, Mama Ang developed diabetes. In prayer, Sian committed all her pains to God her Father and decided to choose ignorance. She had to be strong for her dearest and faithful mother, the only one who saw her from birth, brought her into God's family, and arranged for her marriage to Ah Li. Sian began to realize that though poverty could not choke love, betrayal of trust through infidelity did it. Neverthelesss, somehow, she knew that Ah Li still had a fear of God in his heart. The year before war ended, Ah Li was 34; Sian, 31; Mei Li, 11; Mei Ren, 6 and Ah Keat, 3.

1945 . . . War was over! How did they know? That Friday, when Ah Li took son Ah Keat past the Air Itam cinema hall downhill, they were met with loud celebrative music and British soldiers giving candies, biscuits and chocolates to kids all over the place! At last, peace was here! No more fear, no more curfew, no more potato or tapioca leaves day in and day out! Hurray! All local residents, citizens or immigrants, were so relieved and grateful to those who protected their country and families! The feeling that, *"It's all over, we can start to prosper again!"* filled the air! Freedom at long last! Three years might seem short in peace times but endless when in war! True indeed, that, sometimes, a seed must die in order for fresh shoots to emerge.

As quick as they could, Sian and her family shifted home to their shophouse in Bishop Street, together with hordes of neighbors who had become friends because of war.

At the home front, though unspoken, the children longed to see real reconciliation and peace between their beloved parents but they had to wait. Malaya was already at peace but their home was still at war.

Chapter 8

Calm Before the Storm

Malaya 1945

WWII ended. The British returned. Back at their own home in Bishop Street, Ah Li's family settled down to the bicycle import and export business once more. Yes, they would pick up from where they left before the war. They would do it together as a united family sans the mistress's disruption. She can do what she liked, but she was not part of their family or business. She was Papa Li's problem since he chose to continue the relationship with her. Ah Hoo Ma had explained to Sian when the home front was at war: as God forgave them, they must forgive Ah Li and Chin Chin. Leave God to change their hearts; even devout Mama Ang could not change Ah Li. With this attitude, all at home will know peace and harmony once more. Reluctantly, Sian eventually learned patience through submission to her mother's wise advice in a situation such as hers. She began to see her husband's problem as his problem and not hers. He had to answer to the true Matchmaker, God, before whom he had vowed to his bride, and she to her bridegroom:

"I, Ah Li, take you Sian, to be my wedded wife; to have and to hold, from this day forward, for better or for worse, for richer or for

poorer, in sickness and in health, to love and to cherish till death do us part. And hereto I pledge You my faithfulness.

In the Name of the Father, and the Son and the Holy Spirit, Amen."

and

"I, Sian, take you Ah Li, to be my wedded husband; to have and to hold, from this day forward, for better or for worse, for richer or for poorer, in sickness and in health, to love and to cherish till death do us part. And hereto I pledge You my faithfulness.

In the Name of the Father, and the Son and the Holy Spirit, Amen."

The word *cherish* means *putting the other person top in one's earthly priorities.*

Each made the vow before witnesses, and Ah Hoo Ma was one of them. Sian, though illiterate, began to understand that the public marriage ceremony was not just a ritual or entertaining event but an opportunity for the local community of friends and relatives to hold the young couple accountable for the decision they took on that wedding day. As a psychologist Cline Bell once stated,

"By the community have we been broken, so by the community will we be healed." When their former Pastor Lim officiated their wedding ceremony, he explained thus . . .

". . . That 'no man is an island' was not only the lyrics of a song but a sociological truth in human relations. If the building blocks of any society, primitive or sophisticated, are to fulfill social cohesion, individuals and families need to listen to our relatives, our friends, our elders, our youth and sometimes, even our enemies if their words are to bring oneness and healing among the human marriage, family, church and society. As God is One in the Holy Community of the Father, the Son and the Holy Spirit, so human beings created in His image are to

be one like Him. The difference is that God is perfect, but we are not yet so. But we shall be made perfect one day. Therefore, forgiveness and reconciliation will be a repeated theme in human history for the time being."

Meanwhile, Sian continued to be a faithful wife to Ah Li while persevering to wait for him to cherish her like on the wedding day. As an old saint once prayed, so she prayed:

"Lord, grant me the serenity to accept the things I cannot change, courage to change what I can change, and wisdom to know the difference."

Down the ages, this prayer must have enabled many to live peaceably and joyfully while waiting for perfection to dawn in the universe. Sian's children would call her *Blessed* for keeping the peace at home for them.

Actions could indeed turn him around to his first love for Sian again. She, on the other hand, vowed silently never to have any other man in her life. Some of Ah Li's good friends were widowers due to the war. When they heard of Ah Li's unfaithfulness to such a mature and attractive wife, one of them had tested out her feelings for him. No way, she was a woman of one man till death do them part. Ah Li also did not mention the mistress again and concentrated on providing for his family as best he could, even though his energy and time were now divided. Poor man. It cost him much energy to please two women at the same time. It was just not part of his relaxing leisure. Focusing on building his business was wiser after all.

As Ah Li used his wit to work on growing his company, his income increased several folds. Still, to import Japanese bicycles parts for local assembly needed much capital. He learnt how to make use of overdrafts from banks. Thankfully, he could repay some of the loans each month so that he could borrow some more.

On the home front, since the older girls enrolled in the nearby Convent mission school, contact with teachers who were western nuns had exposed them to a wider world. Though Papa and Mama were not English literate, the girls' chattering in English at home had removed some fear of the *orang puteh* (white people in Malay) from her. Therefore, before their third daughter Mei Lan was born, Ah Li arranged for Sian to have the delivery at the new public Maternity Hospital which was mainly staffed by British or English speaking local doctors and nurses. Suffering through a world war had deepened the trust between colonists and the non-English speaking locals in a manner peace could not do. Both had to survive; one, to return as rulers and the other, to merely stay alive.

Eventually, the family could afford to buy their first car, a dark green British Morris Minor! What a feat for all! Finally, Ah Li fulfilled the one request that his mother-in-law made for her daughter's sake. Sian would have transport all her life. Obediently, Mei Li, Mei Ren, and Ah Keat washed and dried their hands before they were allowed to run their small fingers over the glimmering smooth surface of the bonnet, doors, and boot. When Papa opened the rear door and signaled to them, they scrambled in as fast as they could so much so that their chubby bodies were jammed at the doorway. With Mei Lan in her arms, Mama Ang laughed with joy to watch their antics.

"You'll join them soon, Lan," she said to the baby. "This is God's blessing to us. Thanks, heavenly Father, thanks!"

As the mood lifted even more in the coming year, Sian conceived again. Since domestic helpers were easily available those days and business was good, the family employed a live-in maid for chores and cooking. Sian could then rest more and spend unhurried time with Mei Lan who was hardly ten months old. She was blessed to receive more of Mama Sian's attention as the older three siblings were all in school in the mornings, though Mei Li, Mei Ren, and Ah Keat's education were all delayed one to two years due to the war.

Come mid-1948, Ah Seong, the second son, arrived. Ah Li was elated. Two sons and three daughters . . . what more can a man ask for? Children were a blessing indeed especially when business prospered! But Ah Li wanted to get rich faster.

Every week, without fail, he bought the public lottery tickets. Mei Li was the one who objected since her Sunday School teacher had taught them that buying lottery was a form of gambling.

"I do not want Papa to disobey God because my Sunday School teacher taught us that God does not want us to gamble but to work hard and trust God to give us enough money," she reasoned with her childlike faith.

"I don't want Papa to be punished. I love you very much." But when Papa brushed her off with

"Children should be seen but not heard", she kept her mouth shut over this issue from that time onward.

However, somewhere deep inside, she struggled with whether her teacher or Papa was telling the truth and who to imitate. Traditional Chinese parents of those days did not allow children to discuss differences with them. The talk was just from the top down the generations in many homes. Of course, there were always exceptions.

Two weeks later, Papa Li ran up the stairs again, waving the newspapers in his hands . . . .

"I won, I won, I won third prize in the lottery! It's a shared prize of RM300,000 each!"

However, when Mama Ang heard the good news, immediately she thought,

"O dear, the mistress is not going to leave him now!"

Being a dreamer endowed with an extrovert–intuitive–feeling–flexible personality, ever so often, ideas ran through Ah Li's mind almost uncontrollably: *bigger shop, bigger home, get into the sewing machine business, have more children and on and on.*

But hush, they must not reveal their good fortune to others yet. They must not tempt thieves or kidnappers. Gone were the days when they could let the children play with the neighbors' kids freely and unsupervised on the five-foot-way (a 5 feet wide corridor) in front of the wide shop door. It is strange how a family could become paranoid and anxious overnight, just because of money, out of fear of loss or harm . . . sigh.

However, their instant wealth opened the generous hearts of Ah Li and Sian even wider for good works. They remembered the days of their poverty and willingly shared with those they knew needed cash for schoolbooks, food, or even jobs. In their quiet ways, they did their best. By observing them, their children learnt to also share with those needier than them. If one of Mei Li's classmates came to school with several patches on her uniform, they would inform their parents who would give their form teacher some funds to get new ones for her anonymously. If any of Ah Keat's classmates played on his own at playtime and had no lunch, he would quietly share his lunch with him. The saying, *like father, like son"* or *like mother like daughter"* seemed to be true in this family. One might also add that, *like boss, like employee* was also true as we recall how Ah Li's first boss treated him with abundant charity in his shop-cum-home house in China.

By the end of 1949, Ah Li planned to shift to a bigger space for business and home. Just at the right time, his friend across the street informed him of a ninety feet long shop lot on the same side of the road. He asked to check it out and, to his joy, discovered that it was exactly like what he had in mind. It also belonged to the same owner as the present shop lot. Under the current government rent control laws, the lease was for forty years at a fixed monthly rental of only RM73. Without any hesitation, he closed the deal. After another round of rapid packing up, the family was on the move again though the new shop-cum-home house was just down the road.

1950

Ah Jin, their third and youngest son arrived! Wow, how they celebrated his full moon with firecrackers to give thanks to God for Ah Jin, the new shop and upstairs home and, of course, the largely increased funds for all! By then, they had a live-in nanny for Ah Seong and Ah Jin, a live in cook-cum-cleaner and a washer woman for the daily washing and ironing of clothes and linen. Sian was now a *Towkay-Neoh* (Mrs. Boss in Hokkien) and Mama Ang the *Towkay's* highly respected and beloved mother-in-law. The oldest living person in any Chinese related household had the honor no one else may assume. Overall, Ah Li's family social status had gone up but their modesty remained. What good examples for their younger neighbors.

Having three sons and three daughters now, they were contented. But then Sian began to see that her girls would get married one day. Her sociable Mei Li would most likely marry someone far away as she made friends with many American missionary pastors and teachers; her quiet Mei Ren was good in her studies and would most likely travel overseas too. Mei Lan was too boisterous to stay home. Her boys were like any other boys. When they married, their wives, not their elders, would probably be in charge at home since the westerners they admired so much had that lifestyle. Therefore, when she conceived again at thirty-eight, before the days of ultrasound machines to detect fetal gender, she prayed . . .

"Father, if this one is a girl, she is going to take care of me when I am old and weak. Remember my dislocated hip?"

At 39, Sian's youngest child and fourth daughter was born. She was so glad to receive her. When her older excited children visited her at the Maternity Hospital, and they were not allowed to enter the wards, they shouted from the ground floor garden,

"Mama, Mama, we are outside your window!"

Sian was so excited that she got up from her bed and threw down the bananas, apples, oranges, and toffees she had kept for them! They went wild as they fought to gather the presents in their arms with shouts and squeals!

In summary, at a young thirty-nine years of age, between 1943 and 1952, Sian had nine pregnancies and seven living children aged 19, 15, 12, 5, 4, 2 and newborn! What more can a woman of intelligence, faith, health and wealth ask for, especially when Mama Ang was still with her as her great supporter, peacemaker and friend! The grand elderly matriach was the spiritual and emotional backbone of her young family. Sian was thus determined to be the same to her children.

However, one year later, in 1953, Mama Ang, who always taught her daughter to respect her husband and be an enduring caring considerate wife, fell seriously ill. Due to the complications of diabetes, she had a stroke and a heart attack followed by worsening blindness due to bilateral cataracts. In her last days on earth, she was bedridden and had to be nursed day and night in the upstairs broad open spacious back room at the shophouse home.

When Mama-Grandma Ang died, Sian's moral support crumbled. Ah Li, too, missed her very much. She was the only mother he knew as an adult orphan. She had given her precious daughter to him in trust. He had not cried for years; he did not need to. That night, he mourned in grief.

Chapter 9

Near Death Encounter

Penang 1954

After Grandma's funeral, the first in this small family without close relatives on Sian's side around, Ah Li fell seriously ill. His x-rays showed an inflamed gall bladder cause by several gall stones blocking the ducts. He would roll in agonizing abdominal colicky pain every few weeks after he had fatty food. Pig's trotters braised in dark and light soya source was his favorite dish. When noninvasive methods failed to dislodge or dissolve the stones, the doctor had no choice but to refer him to the surgeon. The first operation to remove the gall bladder and stones was successful. However, internal infection set in and spread fast. The surgeon had to open up the hardly healed surgical wound to drain the pus. When even this did not stop the infection, the doctor informed Sian that he might succumb to the disease. However, a final surgery might arrest the infection. Antibiotics in those days were not as powerful as in our current situation. This last attempt to treat the postoperative infection was his last chance.

What could Sian do with seven children at home aged two to twenty-one years old? Who was there to be her pillar? All of a sudden, the eldest child, Mei Li, seemed to have grown up overnight; she became her strength in making decisions and in driving her between hospital and home two to three rounds a day. During the nights, fourteen year old Ah Keat accompanied Mei Li whenever the hospital called home to inform them of Papa's deteriorating condition. In the day, the company driver would send them. The two siblings spoke English well and were therefore able to translate for Mama. The younger ones were left in the care of maids, shop workers and Mei Ren, seventeen, who was in her public examination year.

Before Ah Li had his third and last surgery where the risk of death was real, he greatly feared an early death at the age of forty-four years. As he reflected on his short life, he realized how much he had hurt the wife of his youth, the lovely Sian. She had suffered enough through his past folly. How was he so insensible to her needs? When he needed her in every way, she was always there as his faithful coworker and wife. He wondered whether she would remarry for the children's sake if he were to die. The very thought of who she could remarry choked him with tears. Surely there would be many older men who would court her as soon as he died. Her beauty and kindness drew old and young to her in the neighborhood and in church. No, he could not stand her remarrying; he still loved her very much. If he were single, he would still choose her to be his wife. He was the envy of many men when he announced their engagement years ago. As he recalled and as he pondered, he became aware of his own wretchedness to have caused her so much suffering in her heart. How could he face God if he were called home today?

Behind the ward bedside curtains that night, alone before the Holy One, he repented in deep sorrow and confessed his sin of adultery to God. Immediately, he felt a heavy burden fell off his shoulders and he promised God that if he were allowed him to live on, he would love Sian all over again. He would love and cherish her. He also promised God something about which even Sian had not yet been told.

In memory of his late parents, he would like to visit his village in mainland China for the first time since he left as a poor orphan. He wanted to share God's blessings with them. No matter what, they were his relatives, his roots. As they lived in poverty in the early days of communist rule while he had so much in Malaya, he must help them.

With a voice hardly audible, he shared his dream of visiting China with Sian. She understood and stood by his dream with him.

The two days before surgery, caring pastors and church members fasted and prayed for Ah Li's healing day and night. Ah Li was deeply touched and uplifted by experiencing God's love through them. He knew that if he were to die, they would be there for Sian.

Then the pastor alerted Ah Li to draw up his will for the family. All were near exhaustion. But a will had to be made to save guard family resources for the wife's and children's daily expenses and education for years to come. It was at this last minute before his critical operation when Papa Li persuaded his right hand business partner, Mei Li, to marry an accountant from a God fearing family, if he did not survive the operation. In this way, she and her future husband could inherit the business to support all at home. He was about to draw up his will there and then. Would she agree?

Mei Li did not have much choice as this instruction was given to her a few minutes before he was to be wheeled into the operating theatre. Either she agreed so that her beloved father could go for a final operation in peace or she disagreed and blamed herself if he were to die on the operating table. What could she do? She simply could not imagine marrying that man. There were some people whom one just could not imagine being with for the rest of one's life! But she also cared for her younger brothers, sisters, and dearest mother.

In dire desperation, she excused herself to use the bathroom in Papa Ah Li's surgical ward. Having been uncertain whether she should answer God's call to study theology for a while, she had been working in Papa's office. Now came the time of reckoning. Without any caution, she knelt on the messy floor, cried to her heavenly Father, the only one who could work miracles, and prayed like never before. She promised God that if He allowed Papa to live, she would obey Him. If he died, then she would take it as a sign to marry that guy, intensely fearful though she was, in order to raise her siblings and support her beloved mother.

Papa lived! He was skin and bones for months as Sian tenderly nursed him back to health. Daily she stewed herbal chicken essence for him; daily she was by his side. When he was mobile and out of danger, they stayed at a hotel by the beach for a month for fresher air and serene surroundings with two year old Mei Tin and four year old Ah Jin tagging along!

What happened to Chin Chin the hairdresser? After ten long years (seemed so much longer to Sian), the authenticity of her love for Ah Li was tested. She failed badly. On secretly hearing of Ah Li's near-death condition, she quietly disappeared. No one in her vicinity ever saw her again. How much had she gained by taking someone's husband and almost breaking up a loving family is anyone's guess. Soon she was out of Ah Li and his family's mind.

Thankfully, business carried on as usual with Mei Li at the helm. They could still afford to keep all the home help and business manual shop workers and driver. The pastor's wife, Mrs. Hsu, provided vital support through her frequent visitations, listening ear, and prayers. What a soothing comfort in times of distress.

When Ah Li recovered completely from the surgery, he resumed his duties as managing director of his import and export trading business.

Then Sian longed to be reunited with his long lost brother, Ah Koh, whom she hoped still lived in Singapore. A few years ago, they sought the Singapore press for help but to no avail. When peace and health reined once more, Sian, being all alone without any close relatives near enough to befriend, asked Ah Li to try looking for them again.

Ah Li was forty-four and Sian was forty-one. All seven children were completely dependent on them still.

Chapter 10

Three Flew Off, Four Left

Penang, Singapore, Australia, America 1957

Once Ah Li was back at his downstairs office, Mei Li gradually released her work to an employed accounts clerk. However, Papa Li refused to let her study theology in order to serve God anywhere He sent. She was beautiful, capable, and fast in her interactions with others. Her father had high regard for her natural skills as a business woman. He would train her through his growing import and export trade dealing with the assembling and sale of Japanese bicycles and sewing machines. There was really no need for her to train in other fields.

Papa Li could not yet understand the reality of God calling someone to do something specific for Him. She was too precious to him to have to serve others instead of being served by maids in their now very comfortable home. Unable to change his mind, Mei Li followed the biblical advice to fast and pray till her father could see the light of her commitment to God, their God. Though it was a testing time for her, she persevered. When her Papa watched how she grew thinner and weaker by the week over thirty days and nights, he gave her his blessings to proceed to attend a seminary Singapore where she would be

68

well taken care of. She seemed to know what she wanted. By then, the family had a branch office in the much larger and more modern city nation. Mei Li was most grateful for Mama Sian who quietly stood by her.

Hence, in January 1957, Ah Li and Sian saw their first child leave home for Singapore. In an era when children seldom venture beyond their hometowns, Ah Li and Sian struggled with the release of their eldest much loved daughter who was going so far away for two years. However, the period of preparation for the moment of farewell gave them a sense of parental fulfillment and tears at the same time. But Singapore seemed so far away for Penangites then; it felt as far as China! Mei Li later recalled how Mama Sian and she broke into tears as soon as the returning railway ferry's horn tooted long, hollow and clear . . .

'Toooooot'!

It was a sign to give one another a last hug before they left Mei Li at the Prai railway station while they returned to Penang Island. Little Mei Tin recalled how she watched the adults with apprehension and picked up the cue to cry during future good-byes. She hated farewells since then. This emotional response to separation from a significant someone in life could cause havoc in later family life if not diagnosed and healed. It could even develop into a pathological grief syndrome in adult life. For then, in the next few months, she consciously experienced what it means to miss someone dear to her. In the afternoons, when her older siblings had their own things to do, Mei Tin would cry softly while grasping and smelling her Big Sister Mei Li's blanket, her *Linus' blanket*. She was more bonded to her than the other siblings as Big Sister babysat her the most, feeding her with handrolled rice balls. When she was taking too long with her meals, occasionally, Big Sister slipped a tiny bit of hot *chilly padi* (a species of biting hot chilly) into the rice ball and baby sister would gobble up her food real fast! How she missed her Big Sister . . . she would rather have the chilly than not to have her again!

Nevertheless, the missing of Mei Li at home, by all, was soon overridden by the long awaited locating of Sian's Big Brother, Ah Koh, in Singapore. But Sian was too busy with her home affairs to arrange for a reunion yet.

After the home front normalized again, it was time to prepare Mei Tin, six, for kindergarten. January 1958 saw the youngest of the seven children taking a bold step into the brave new world! In addition, it was also the first time Sian had no one at home to babysit in the mornings since her first baby was born twenty-five years ago.

Further, in February 1958, Mei Ren flew to Melbourne for her university undergraduate course in government, economics, and psychology. Come August the same year, Ah Keat dreamt of pursuing a degree in nuclear physics. However, as it was the days of the cold war and not long after Hiroshima, Papa Ah Li stopped him from pursuing his dream. Eventually, he left for America to pursue a course in liberal arts at Harvard University, which led him to a highly successful medical career. Ah Keat, his eldest son, had made him proud.

So who remained at home with Ah Li and Sian?

The four more relaxed sons and daughters born after WWII, of course.

Happy parents make happy children. All four attended school; soon they would leave home too! Sian was very determined to see all her children be educated as much as they could so that they would not be trapped in illiteracy like she was.

For now, it was time for Ah Li to remember his roots. He discussed his wish with Sian as they recalled their earlier conversation when he was hospitalized. Though Sian, born and bred in Singapore and then lived in Malaya, had never set foot on Chinese soil, she wholeheartedly agreed! Her husband's relatives were hers as well. She would go with him if she could.

Chapter 11

To China with Love

Penang, China 1959

In late 1958, Ah Li and Sian began to make plans for a trip back to China. However, Sian would not travel with him this time due to her concern for their four small younger children. Reluctantly, Ah Li agreed. He would be there for only two weeks. If there were no emergency situations, he would definitely be home for the 1959 Chinese New Year. Then the whole household commenced the hectic preparation for the return of Ah Li to his people! On the side of his mainland China relatives, the return of a prosperous orphan lifted their expectations for rewards. They viewed anyone who came out of the village as theirs. Were they not the ones who saw him run around in his uncle's house? Were they not the ones who helped watch over him when his parents died? Ah Li had occasionally sent monetary gifts to them; now they wanted more, though no one could even guess how they would try to make him return again and again to be an asset to them regardless of his current true home in Malaya.

In Penang, when someone passes wind, as they say till today, everyone knows! All their Chinese family friends knew about this important trip for Ah Li. They understood the significance of an orphan's return to his roots. It would mean a lot to him as a first generation overseas Chinese. His uncles, aunties, nephews, and nieces would be so proud of him. Ah Li had also planned to dig a new well for them and build two classrooms to add to their few old ones. Therefore, some even offered him gifts of money in red packets as farewell gifts. Others simply lent moral support by cheering him on as they watched the children and workers help pack boxes of men and women's clothing, electrical good, household utensils, hardy bags, and even nail clippers. Mei Lan, Ah Seong, Ah Jin, and Mei Tin enjoyed those days most of all! After school hours, they joined in the crowd and at times were more in the adults' way than a help! But they stayed on in the shop area to watch even if they could not get nearer. This had its bonus for when some boxes were too full for more goods to be packed in, the remaining goodies, such biscuits and toys, were given to them. What fun for two whole weeks! Ah Li's fellow businessmen were happy for his family and him and wished him bon voyage the Chinese way. They gave him a hearty ten course Hokkien dinner, the night before he left, at the local Chinese restaurant, with many rounds of "*Yam Seng*" ("*Cheers*")!

In January 1959, having promised Sian that he would write, Ah Li finally left on a cargo ship which was sailing to Hong Kong. From there, he would take a twohour train ride to Amoy. His cousins would meet him there with a truck to bring all his gifts home to their village, another two hours away on the road. Their relatives were anxiously anticipating his return as the rich son of his late parents. Would Ah Li's peers recognize him? How many of his older relatives would still be there?

Meanwhile, time passed slowly in Bishop Street without the presence of the head of the family. Furthermore, no letter came from Ah Li. Sian daily waited for the postman to bring Ah Li's mail but to no avail. She wondered why. Was he safe?

Those were the early years of communist rule in China with many horror stories coming out to overseas Chinese. Hopefully, he was just too busy helping his people repair the village school and dig a new well for them.

Fourteen days flew by and still no mail came. Papa Li was supposed to be home before the first day of the Chinese New Year. It was already the twenty-eighth day of the twelfth moon of the Chinese lunar year but there was no news or sign of him yet.

A cloud of silent uncertainty hung over Sian.

Sian tried to keep her anxiety from the children, but they sensed her mood and behaved very well at home. She prayed for Ah Li. Her pastor and friends prayed with her. When Sian could wait no longer, she sent their manager to the neighboring business friends opposite their shop to enquire from mutual friends for her.

A bomb dropped! Bad news. Someone, who was on the same ship as Ah Li on the forward trip and had come back. He heard a rumor while in a village nearby to his. Ah Li had taken another wife from the neighboring Tan village. Apparently, as soon as he reached his village, his uncles taunted him for marrying an overseas born Chinese wife from Malaya. In their tradition, they said, she was not regarded as his legitimate wife. He must marry a village girl of their own background. Hence, they wanted to matchmake him with a single lady to be his authentic Chinese wife. The temptation was too strong for him. He took in their reasoning and forgot about his God, his loving waiting wife Sian and his seven children back home. Finally, Ah Li took the lady as his *legitimate wife* in the eyes of his relatives.

Ah Li showered rich gifts to all villagers at the traditional marriage ceremony. The village elders persuaded him to live in China permanently to show his loyalty to his ancestors and his clan. That was why he delayed his departure from his village.

When his relatives kept asking him for money, Ah Li suddenly came to his senses and remembered that his wealth came from his business in Penang—his one and only genuine home. He could not survive in communist China. He would better take the next boat south, back to his shop and family.

Of course, Sian could not believe her ears. Holding her heart in her hands and, as if transported to another world, she thought to herself, *How could it be? He would not do this to me again after all the trials we went through together during his illness! Maybe they heard wrong.*

Another week passed, and, finally, Ah Li stepped into their shophouse upstairs home. All was quiet. All ate in silence that night. No one asked any question. The four children received their presents from Papa without jumping up and down with glee. Sian took them to their rooms and went straight to bed.

In the middle of the night, Mei Lan, now the eldest of the four children at home, was woken up by the hair raising scream of a woman from Papa and Mama's bedroom. It was her Mama's voice. Papa had just confessed to Mama about the mistress left in China. The confirmation of her suspicion knocked her hard. Her hope that the rumor was false was dashed. She went into a state of shock! One could not imagine the knife-like pain in the heart of a wife who had just discovered her husband's betrayal unless she had experienced it before. For months, Sian cried while Ah Li pined for his lover far away. After dinner each night, he stayed up at his ground floor office to write love letters to his mistress till long after midnight. If Sian persuaded him to come upstairs to sleep, he shooed her away for disturbing him. He started to switch off lights early in the evening because in China, they were bereft of twenty-four hour electricity; the family must be thrifty because the mistress was poor and so on.

How Sian grieved for her husband's love, how she daily cried with a pain which felt like that of having a heart attack, how she despaired of ever being strong enough to live on. Her three older children, who could understand her better, were too far for her to call and too expensive for them to come back there and then. She was not English literate while they were in English speaking countries. Mei Li was having her examinations in Singapore which seemed very far to her. Sian's home was her world! She felt so helpless and contemplated taking her life or asking God to take it away but for her younger four children who still needed her for years to come.

It was a severe tragedy that broke Sian's heart a second time, so soon after it was healed!

Meanwhile, each afternoon, after returning from kindergarten, six year old Mei Tin lay beside her dear mother on her bed and watched her Mama's agonizing controlled sobs. *Mama was like Jesus crying in the Garden of Gethsemane,* she thought, recalling the story her Big Sister Mei Li told her last Good Friday. Mei Tin asked no question; she simply absorbed her Mama's pains. No wonder that Mei Li's adult memory of her childhood was one of sadness. Her innocent and carefree life was gone at six because Papa publicly broke his marriage vows to her Mama and refused to say sorry to Mama. Shame and false guilt filled her innocent soul!

For children, what could be worse than being torn apart by severe parental conflicts?

Ah Li's impulsive actions affected all his seven children badly. They developed a fear of being around him as he would get into a rage whenever Sian persuaded him to leave the mistress. Though he kept his promise to his late mother-in-law to always care for Sian and therefore never lifted a finger on her, he was sometimes violent to even his adult kids when he felt that they were on Sian's side. Yet which normal thinking son or daughter would agree with sharing their Papa or Mama with another woman or man in their lives? Family life in their household would never be the same again for a long long time to come. Gratefully, all maids and workers also empathized with Sian. She needed their comfort and affirmation that she was not wrong to feel angry. If they had condemned her for not trying hard enough to keep her husband, it could have driven her to attempt suicide. God was also on her side, she knew.

Finally, after several months of intense tension at home, to compensate Sian, Ah Li sent Sian and Mei Tin to be reunited with Ah Koh in Singapore. He must be waiting for his long lost sister too. Ah Li also gave Sian a large sum of money for the trip. He felt that he could part with money when he had it, but not a mistress. Deep inside, he wanted Sian, but he had placed himself in a trap too strong for him. Sian really needed the comfort of a big brother even though they had not met for decades. She, of all in the family, needed a total break from home. Ah Li arranged for his Singapore manager to pick them up and take them to visit Ah Koh.

On arrival at big brother's house in crowded *Ang Moh Keow*, Sian and Mei Li climbed up the dark and narrow staircase of a three-storey shophouse to get to Ah Koh's top floor. That was his home with Ah Chan, his wife, and their adult children. It was so depressing to discover that Ah Koh was bedridden due to suffering from a stroke the previous year. Physiotherapy was unknown in their culture then. Out of ignorance and tradition, an invalid was kept immobile and thus became even weaker. To do everything for them is to care for them as an invalid. That was the way to show gratitude and love to the elderly. To encourage such a patient to exercise was like punishing him. As they sipped hot coffee, they recounted their missing of each other.

Sian asked about Papa Saw, her late father, while Ah Koh asked about Mama Ang, his long lost *"Aboo"* (*Mum* in traditional Hokkien). On discovering on how both their parents had died years back, they mourned loudly in grief and regretted at being too late to see them alive again! But, at least, they had found one another and that was a great comfort indeed. They were also very glad to know that both were married and had filial children. Again, little Mei Tin watched and heard in fear as the bedroom was dinghy; she felt hemmed in. Then, almost immediately, her older cousins gently led her out to the lounge and showered her with pretty dresses, a gold necklace and bracelet, boxes of biscuits and colorful hair pins! They knew what a six-year-old girl liked and had gone shopping when they knew that a much younger cousin was visiting for the first time! It felt really great to be the youngest at times.

On returning to Penang, Sian was so thrilled to be reunited with her one and only brother that, for a while, Sian and the children could laugh again, especially when Papa was not home.

Chapter 12

Guts and Grace

Penang 1959

In spite of the emotional turmoil, 1959-1971 saw Sian's younger four younger ones pass through childhood into adolescence and adulthood. A mother's love protected them from a harsh father due to his meandering ways. Most major decisions required for the four came from Ah Li to them through Sian, and their requests to their father went in the reverse direction through her. However, the children knew that Papa Li had a soft spot for all his children. He loved children; he wanted to be the best father and give them the best education and daily needs. But they feared his rage when the issue of his extramarital affair surfaced at any time. Ah Li was too pre-occupied with the mistress and other women in his life and had lost sight of the meaning of commitment to only one family. He also cancelled the weekly Bible reading and prayer times at home.

Since he left his village in search of freedom from his uncle, he failed to see the freedom he already had as an orphan in terms of parental control. He misunderstood self-will as freedom. He eventually weaved a trap for himself that hindered that tangibility of true freedom. Neither did he really care for the other women apart from Sian and his children. He used them to satisfy his own needs, not theirs as well, though he could discuss wider issues with Ah Tan, the China mistress as she was literate. However, her literacy caused much self-doubt in Sian. In her agony, she wondered whether Ah Li preferred Ah Tan because of her inability to read and write. But any outsider would vouch that this was not the reason as.

In better times, Ah Li used to patiently read aloud the daily news to Sian whenever he was reading the newspapers. From those readings, she knew what was going on in the world during the cold war period between the USSR and America. She knew about the Indonesia–Malaysia conflicts and how it impacted Malaysia. She knew geography because her husband read the daily news to her. Sian wanted to believe he loved her as he was usually gentle to her. It was only his wayward heart that she could not grasp. That was his secure territory where no one was allowed to trespass. He was so blinded by self-will that he could not see even God anymore. He had not only broken his marriage vows, he had broken his baptismal vows before God as well. This gave the local church no choice but to ex-communicate him after several gentle and loving attempts to win him back through repentance and reconciliation with God, family, and the fellowship of His people. He had committed adultery in public and publicly claimed to be right.

It broke Sian's heart when Ah Li's name was struck off the church membership register. Church was their second home and she needed to be there with her children. However, the sense of shame due to Ah Li's sins was too heavy for her. She continued to carry his burden of guilt and shame. Therefore, she temporarily worshipped with another congregation where the migrant mainland China pastor and his wife accepted her warmly with deep compassion for a woman betrayed by her husband. To be understood and befriended by a godly traditional Chinese pastoral couple was culturally healing indeed. However, the four children remained in the fellowship of the first church where friendships among youth were strong. They never discuss home problems with each other at all. They simply suffered silently. Mei Tin was especially affected as she followed Mama everywhere whenever she needed her for company while Mama ran her errands at shops or banks. This was so through all her twelve years of school. Once, when Mama first felt a sudden and severe pain in her dislocated hip, she gripped Mei Li for instant support. To an eleven-year-old girl, the fear of having to physically support her aging mother laid an unshakeable burden on her heart.

"If I don't want Mama to die, then I must take care of her ..." was her subconscious motto.

From then on, she prayed that one day, when she grew up, she would take care of Mama and bring her joy! God answered both Mama's and Mei Tin's prayer ..."*If this one is a girl, she is going to take care of me.*" It was just that Mei Tin did not know then that it was going to be so hard on her.

After a few years, Sian returned to their home church. Life carried on at home. Most of Sian's waking hours were spent in supervising the four children's ins and outs, namely, their studies, ballet, piano or violin lessons, various tuition classes, and a host of other teenage activities such as getting in and out of infatuations, though most of those tales were kept secret from her. What were the youngest four children like?

Mei Lan

Strong, verbose, and creative in her own ways, Mei Lan grew up into one of the most rebellious of Penang teenagers. In the 1960s, when girls seldom cycled out of home at any time or went anywhere without parental permission, Mei Lan was a pioneer in going against traditional cultural norms. Since Papa sold bicycles, there were a few parked in the long shophouse. Near dinner time, when Mama yelled out that dinner was ready, she could go hoarse waiting for her reply. Why? She preferred the 30 cents worth of ladies' fingers soaked in milky Indian curry to the maid's delicious dishes. She would cycle off on her own to get it or she would just order the worker to go buy some for her and ate before or after the rest of the family. At seventeen, when she decided not to continue her secondary school studies, she simply sold off her newly bought uniform to her classmates. That was Mei Lan for you. She was the only who managed to keep Mama Sian on her toes most of the time.

Old family friends used to call her *How Lam* (*a professional mourner* in Hokkien) because every time she dropped by, Mei Lan was throwing a temper tantrum by crying and kicking her restless legs while on the floor! On hindsight, she could be missing Grandma Ang so much as the latter spent most time with her while Mama Sian was busy with other things, for example, having frequent pregnancies and supervising workers in the shop. Perhaps those were mere signs of a deep need for attention due to unhealed grief for Grandma. Of course, nobody at home understood psychology (the systematic study of the science of the human mind and emotions which commenced in the western world of research) those days. Hence, Mei Lan was not helped at all but was classified as a naughty child! However, she did change when a handsome young businessman appeared, courted and married her. It was the good beginning of a new and happy life for her and for her maiden family.

Ah Seong

Quiet and intelligent, Ah Seong liked to fool around with Ah Jin, especially when Papa was absent from the house. As the shophouse was so long that it had two sets of staircases, they played cowboy and red Indian by chasing each other up and down those strong wooden stairs with harmless wooden rulers in their hands as hammers or guns. Together, they took classes in Chinese martial art while little sister Mei Tin tagged along and imitated their moves. Some evenings, when the man shop workers, who stayed downstairs, took their evening stroll to the nearby banking and jetty areas, they usually took Ah Seong with them. A friendly Punjabi neighbor who worked at the nearest banks liked to carry him while he basked in the old man's attention. Such was the simple trusting Malayan friendship bonds of those days.

Ah Jin

Endowed with more height than the rest of the male members of his family at that age, Ah Jin also had the most childlike and yet aggressive personality in childhood. Once, when his father's worker teased him, he held up a real hammer and threatened to hit the older man if he should come nearer to him. Thus, his nickname was *Red Indian*. English storybooks, for some reason, often depicted Red Indians as men who held tomahawks in their uplifted hands. How unfair people could be. Yet didn't all imperfect beings, at some time or other, blindly subscribe to such unfair labeling of people?

These are examples of stereotypes, which are now being increasingly rejected by twenty-first century global citizens. People all over the world have become more aware that God created men and women as equals, though they might have different temperaments with unique functions. Stereotypes might be of use as illustrations but not in building friendly relationships across the world. Men and women were indeed born to be peacemakers, not trouble makers.

Mei Tin

Being the last of seven strong willed, creative and adventurous siblings, Mei Tin knew what and when to say something at home. The skill came naturally to her through intuition and the daily observation of her elders and was much needed if she were to survive. She was told in no uncertain terms that she had eight, not two heads in authority over her, namely, father, mother, three elder brothers and three elder sisters. She had to submit to them when a disagreement surfaced. At that position in the family, she had the unenviable/enviable (depending on what one is looking for) role of watching everyone live and perform from her corner. She does not consider herself spoilt but liked and loved by her parents and six older siblings as long as she obeyed them!

Sensitive and intuitive Mei Tin learnt, through the hard way, to avoid conflicts by staying away from the three eldest overseas siblings when they came home on vacation. However, she disliked Mama's rule that, no matter who was right or wrong, the younger always had to apologize and talk to the older first, after a cold war. That was just not fair! Her acute sense of fairness sometimes caused her prolonged suppressed anger to eventually develop into a type of passive resistance and perfectionistic thought pattern. But as she grew older and wiser from learning how God related with imperfect humans in the Bible, she began to accept her imperfections and that of others and thus lived a freer, more balanced and joyful adult life in later years!

Some of her later hang ups were due to her seeing her elder siblings leave home but never returning to help care for their aging parents, especially when Papa's business went downhill, and there were more quarrels at home due to Papa having to support two families. At that stage, she could not understand that grown ups sometimes had their other duties to fulfill. Yet, nearing old age, Papa and Mama loved their four younger children enough to always reassure all of them that, as long as they studied well, they would find the necessary funds for them for their tertiary education. It was not their problem to look for funds. Papa and Mama did not leave the four younger ones to be mentally stressed by their fear of a lack of funds. They wanted them to follow their older siblings' footsteps in achieving higher education. They were loyal parents indeed.

Eventually, Mei Li, Mei Ren, and Ah Keat finally graduated, met their respective beloveds, got married, and ventured out to start their respective family by faith! The children had learnt that commitment was the glue of any marriage. It was definitely not beauty, riches, health or degrees, and status in society. When all were married and had children, whenever marriage or parenting trials became near intolerable, it was the memory of their parents' commitment to them that greatly coaxed them to forgive and reconcile again and again and again with their own spouses and children. It was Mama Sian's commitment *not* to separate from Papa that encouraged the sisters and brothers to be committed to their respective spouse till death do them part.

Yes, they had differences and struggles, but divorce was not in their marriage and family vocabulary. So the children were kept safe till they built their own homes. Building a love house was hard for anyone indeed! But Sian's modeling of perseverance helped them continue doing so for their children, not by guts but by grace (God's mercy, which no one is worthy of and no one can manage to earn at all).

While Papa Ah Li was an extroverted, intuitive, feeling and flexible individual while Mama Sian was introverted, sensing, thinking and more rigid. Their natural gifts of temperament seemed to have flowed to their children by their willingness to change with the times of the 1960s era. They both adapted well to the music and fashion of their younger four teenagers who, therefore, enjoyed the freedom to be themselves while still in their parents' nest. By then, Malaya had also grown into Malaysia in September 1963.

When the British were around before the Malayan independence from British rule in 1957, Papa took the initiative to learn a speckle of English phrases in order to join in the businessmen's appeal for Penang to become a free port. He needed that as he imported Japanese goods. Though he could not speak much of the new language, he knew enough to understand if translators made mistakes. They could not cheat him.

Ah Li also gave what he enjoyed to his children, for example, in days when there was only the Cold Storage Supermarket on Penang Island, Papa bought creamy ice-cream and kraft cheese for the younger ones to try out. Though he had no idea what western classical music entailed, he sent them for lessons in that genre of music. When Mei Tin wanted violin and ballet lessons, he encouraged her. In addition, when he returned from business in Japan, he came home with Japanese music records and taught them traditional Japanese dances and songs. From Bangkok, he brought home diamonds; from Jakarta and Medan, Indonesian tomatoes and rendang beef (one type of curry cooked in thick coconut milk); from Taiwan and Hong Kong, pearls of the orient and rich Chinese herbs.

Therefore, though traditional by upbringing, Ah Li was a global modern man in his own rights through the need to survive. Somehow, he was able to break through the gender bias for the male stronghold in Asian traditions to regard and treat all his sons and daughters equally by granting them the opportunities they needed to blossom in this world, long before human rights and gender issues became public in Malaysia. Are not first-generation overseas Chinese true adventurers and entrepreneurs, each in their own corner and in their own quiet ways?

Sian, on the other hand, liked being at home to potter around. In her own ways, she socialized with neighbors, relatives, and friends. Her home was always open to those who needed a listening ear, and her purse, to the needy.

Someone said that when God created each person, He broke the mold. How true it had been for Ah Li and Sian. Though vastly different, they learnt to live together for their children's sake, for better or for worse. Therefore, in the last days of their lives on earth, their children rose up to give them honor and praise. However, due to the width of exposure at various stage of their parents' lives, when the seven siblings compared notes of their childhood days at home in Penang, the older three pre-war kids seemed to have been brought up in a different family from the younger post-war four. They laughed together and thanked God for their parents and each other for all their beauty and their scars. Truly, God could and did make all things work together for the good of those who loved Him and were called according to His purpose indeed!

Sian's faith in her God held her sane all those years. When she did not hear from Ah Li during one of his trips overseas when the youngest four were still in primary school, she panicked and wondered whether his airplane had crashed. The evening news reported on such a crash about the time he was to return. Before dinner, as she sat outside the shophouse for some fresh air and to ponder, she looked up at the sky and saw clouds in the shape of a cross. Instantly, she knew that Ah Li would come home safely. Mama Sian shared her experience with Mei Tin who was thus certain of the reality and nearness of her mother's God and her God, though she was literate but not Mama.

When Mei Li was twelve, she fainted at home and broke her right jaw bone. While she was in the treatment chair of the dental clinic at the Penang General Hospital, Mama waited outside, afraid of what was happening behind doors. All of a sudden, Mama heard angels singing a hymn from a window adjacent to the clinic door,

"What a friend we have in Jesus, all my griefs and pains to bear . . ." in Hokkien.

Immediately, she knew that Mei Tin was safe, and the surgical–dental procedure on her would be successful. What a gift of faith for one so afraid of praying in public. No high power debate could rob her of the certainty of her heavenly Father and her Friend!

The lyrics of an old hymn, titled "He", often reminded her of the power of God's forgiveness without which on one could be redeemed from their past to be God's friends.

God indeed is indeed gracious, fair, and loving to all. Nothing could shake that reality in Mei Tin. But His was not cheap grace; it was grace through the sacrifice of His beloved Son who died on the cross for the sins of the whole world.

As Mei Tin was the scribe and translator for her parents' correspondence with their overseas children, she could feel with Papa and Mama' struggles of faith when they were aging and days were gloomy. This faith in the unchanging all good and all powerful God kept her through her own temptations and trials in the later years of being confronted by secularism (in Australia, Britain and America in the 1970s) and its offspring of amorality. Sadly, Mei Tin also had to contend with the twenty-first century phenomenon of an increasingly secularized Malaysia of today.

However, being also imperfect, Sian sometimes vented her frustration on her children when Ah Li carried on with his affairs, seducing, dancing, and carousing till the wee hours of the night. The children hence grew up with deep emotional wounds in their hearts. The seven kids, near and far, suffered silently and were loyal to Mama Sian but respected and cared for both. The fear of being further hurt by their father dug deep into their lives. The kids feared him due to his banning anyone from mentioning his infidelity to Sian. If they do, they would be slapped or chased out of the room. That was his second biggest mistake. Yet he was generous when business was good and was open to the western creative arts, though he did not grow up with such a culture.

It was not surprising then, that Mei Tin grew up praying that one day, she would tell all fathers never to make their Papa's mistakes in having more than one woman in their lives as such action really caused unnecessary hurts in both their wife and children just as much!

In the growing family of Ah Li and Sian, the grace of forgiveness softens, heals, comforts, and redeems while guts gave them the determination to move on with increasing joy and peace, come what may. God's gifts are good indeed.

Chapter 13

Empty Nest

Penang, Australia, United Kingdom 1966

Ah Li and Sian's youngest four children flew off from their Penang nest between 1966 and 1971.

Mei Lan, the fifth child but the oldest and gang leader of the four youngest post-WWII kids, was allergic to studies. Instead, she took up the trade of selling insurance. She became a successful insurance agent in Penang, got married to her childhood sweetheart and insisted that she too went overseas as her married home was across the narrow channel from Penang Island. It was a popular and value loaded concept, in the Penang of the 1970s, to have *gone overseas*. It gave one who had lived overseas (which usually meant the more developed countries in the west) great pride as if he or she had been to a better place, had a better education and had a better of everything, that is, except that of being more filial to parents and more faithful to one's spouse! It was normal to hear the following stories . . .

"You know, white people divorce their wife or husband easily. Worse than that, they send their old parents to nursing homes when their parents could not take care of themselves any longer."

Of course, the Asians then did not know that this was going to be the case in modern developing twenty-first century

Malaysia as well! They also did not know that many filial white people existed and nursed their parents in their own homes then. It took people who have traveled and witnessed various communities in the world, whether in the east or the west, before they could calm down and accept the fact that it was the hearts of humans that matter, not their skin color. We have decent moral religious and spiritual people in every nation; we also have indecent, immoral/amoral irreligious unspiritual people in all nations. It was and still is any retired couple's dream (especially that of wives of busy husbands) that when they grow older, they would have more time for each other, to read and to follow hobbies. But this was not to be the case for Sian and Ah Li due to the presence of a third party. Sian could not because Ah Li had to provide for the other family. He was often short of money as business declined.

After independence, the Malaya and then Malaysia gradually increased import taxes in order to build up more local enterprise. The free port status of the Penang port eventually ended. Furthermore, the government raised the import tax for imported bicycle tyres in order to encourage the sales of locally produced ones. Having squandered much of his wealth through his frivolous living, Ah Li did not have much savings to tide him through the Malaysian economic transition. He became irritable whenever his bankers and creditors knocked on his shop door.

One by one, his helpless children studied hard in order to leave for overseas universities. Only Mei Lan saw marriage as her freedom, and she was practical and worldly wise. Sian knew that too. Hence, she held on to her savings for years so that if Ah Li could not afford to send them, she would. Once financially independent, they could care for her in later years. She would travel while she had health; she would visit them without having to feel trapped by Ah Li's idiosyncrasies and foolish living. However, it would be difficult for her to travel on her own due to her damaged hip and her state of illiteracy (which she termed *blindness*). Since her oldest three children left home, she had to depend on Mei Tin, who was English educated, or friends, to write or read letters for her. For many years, her children were her only long term pen pals across the seas.

Meanwhile, Mei Tin had to experience the increasingly depressive mood at home of poorer quality food placed on the dining table each day, the sale of the better of two family cars, the closing of the main shop front as business dwindled and the retrenchment of workers one by one till only a new boy was employed to run errands. But, thankfully, Mama still had the one run down first model of the Toyota for her use. Papa had kept his word to Mama's mother and her.

Gladly and timely, Ah Seong left for Perth in 1967, Ah Jin for America in 1969 and Mei Tin for UK in 1971. Sian discouraged the six children from returning so that they did not have to bear Ah Li's burdens except for one. Silently, she hoped that Mei Tin would return to take care of her if she could not, one day, adjust to temperate climates where five of her children lived. With a medical degree, Mei Tin would be able to support and provide her with a maid, should she become an invalid. However, her hope seemed dashed as Mei Tin broke the news to her that she was going to marry an eligible young teacher who was training to become a Christian minister or pastor.

"What?" she reacted in shock!

"How could she marry someone who has chosen to be poor when she has a bright future before her?"

"Will they be able to take care of their children and me?"

Suddenly, the old fears of being abandoned caused an emotional tsunami in her life near old age! She had underestimated her youngest daughter's love for God and her commitment to care for her. This understandable anxiety took root in her heart that day when Mama landed on Mei Tin's arm helplessly, with great fear in her eyes. Neither could Mei Tin understand till decades later, why she automatically and naturally knew she wanted to return to care for Mama. But, in their family, the voice of the youngest was not to be heard. Hence, she had kept her commitment all to herself. Only her God and her future husband knew. She had learnt through a statement of Billy Graham, the humble worldwide evangelist, that:

"God works in mysterious ways, His wonders to behold!"

That was sufficient for her to go on loving God and fellowman even when the going got tough.

Nevertheless, Mei Tin never saw marriage as her outlet. It was education that would bring freedom of the mind and life! As soon as she could, she hoped to help the needy and suffering know God and fulfill His dreams. That was the reason she chose to marry a future pastor even when there were other suave Christian men who courted her. But could her beloved mother understand?

Chapter 14

The Tussle of Priorities

Penang, United Kingdom 1978

Mei Tin, a doctor at twenty-five, married Cheng at twenty-six, against her beloved mother's unspoken will.

"Why does not Mum support my marrying a future pastor when she was overjoyed for Mei Li to do so?" agonized the youngest and most loved child.

The backdrop, as we know by now, was that of a once poor overseas Chinese woman who became middle-class through sheer hard work. Her love and loyalty had nurtured and provided for her kids to outgrow their lowly circumstances. Therefore, she saw marriage of a richer woman to a poorer man as taking several steps backwards from success and pride in her concept of parenting abilities.

The other factor was her intense hidden fear of being left alone in a lurch, especially when she suffered from a left hip weakness. She knew that her children who have emigrated would not return just for her sake. They had their own lives to live. Didn't she bring them up to be successful? Neither could she go to them. Did she not try to live with her eldest son Ah Keat's westernized family a few years ago when the Penang nest was empty? She appreciated their welcome and acceptance but she just did not know what to do when living in Boston. Alien to the American English language except for a *hello* and *bye-bye*, being cooped up in the centrally heated comfortable and big house was definitely not her cup of tea. She used to be so independent and active before. She could not make telephone calls either as it was just too expensive. The American lifestyle was just not for her. So home she came to Penang!

Mei Tin had not verbalized to her mother her desire to take care of her as such as they were miles apart during her student and working days in the UK. But she was determined to do so. When her boyfriend proposed to her, she even took his willingness to help her care for her mother as a sign for her consent to marry him. How could anyone leave a weak elderly mother alone to live in a less than happy peaceful environment? She deserved all the peace and happiness in old age. She believed that one who loved God would honor her parents by caring for them when needed. Mama Ang was the woman closest to her heart from conception right through her formative years. Mei Tin grew up watching her mother's every movement, smelling her every breath, feeling her every heartbeat while sitting on her lap many afternoons. She daily heard Mama's voice for eighteen and a half years. Mama Ang's character and personality must have been deeply ingrained into hers.

Before leaving home for her tertiary education, Mei Tin had asked God for two things:

1. *That Mama Sian would live to see her graduate and return to take care of her since Mama was not happy to stay with Papa*
2. *That Mama could live with her so that they could serve God together.*

God answered both prayers! Why then was Sian so disappointed over Mei Tin's marriage?

To become prosperous is one major Chinese dream. Prosperity, symbolized by the red color, is vaguely defined as being blessed with many children and the following generations to have much food, money, and personal health. Just like many Chinese parents, she feared poverty, which would mean lack of medical health care; she feared suffering alone and she feared personal negligence by loved ones, whether the residence was luxurious or not.

She also knew that the parsonage was a home to which those in need of spiritual and emotional stress would come. However, when things turned bad, the pastoral couple was often to be blamed. Had she not been friends to many pastoral couples before? She was kind to each of her pastors' family in earlier days? She smiled as she recalled how she gave them the best dishes of home cooked food and baked pastry at every Chinese and Christian celebration. Anyone sending the food to the pastor must repeat exactly what she dictated, that is,

"Pastor, Mrs. Ah Li has some food for you to savor."

They had to be polite and generous to the pastoral family who knew God better than them. Pastors worked hard and sacrificially for the Lord; therefore, the people must help to take care of their families. But the pastor was also often at the beck and call of those he served. Further, perpetually being peacemakers between difficult members might eventually wear them down emotionally. Sian honored them a lot. However, she never ever thought that her beloved daughter would be chosen by God to marry one!

"That is asking too much, Lord!"

It was true and still is in the hearts of many Christian parents who themselves had not understood what a calling from God was about. It was a command by One in complete authority over His people's lives. Hence, His specific and unique order for each of His children surely demanded a clear response.

"Either I obey or I die!" was how one who had been specifically called by God to fulfill a specific task felt, if they were willing to obey Him.

However, the prayer *"Lord, call their children, not mine!"* has become a common but serious joke among naive Christians.

Further, Sian also knew that, having gone through hardship as a younger lady, she brought up Mei Tin to live a comfortable life with maids at home, just like how Ah Li and she had brought her up. Therefore, since Mei Ti could afford to provide for herself and her mother to live a life of comfort and plenty, why not? It would be an utter waste of her training and Sian's hard-earned savings if, one day, due to her husband's busyness, she had to quit her medical work to be at home with their children. Her youngest daughter just was not prepared to become a pastor's wife! She would have no emergency savings of her own.

"I don't want her to suffer!" she asserted to one of her older children over a long distance call one day.

Thankfully, her older children knew that Mei Tin's husband, Cheng, was of a good character and of an intelligence at least equivalent to that of their little sister. All of them liked his personality and had no problem with his vocation. They have traveled far and knew what life in the outside world was like ... even in the 1970s. They were quietly glad that their spouses were fully accepted by their parents several years ago as they married those of their parents' expectations!

In Asian cultures, the extended family could cause much sorrow and confusion of priorities to the young couple's marital life if the couple's commitment to cherish each other above all else, except God, were not strong in the first place. Many stayed married unhappily; many also learned to give and take, which is the art of negotiations in any relationship.

Consequently, how did Mei Tin respond to her mother's attitude?

Being submissive to the will of God and His ways, though she at times secretly cried her heart over this matter (since she did not wish to sadden her husband or her mother), she has learnt to forgive till she lost count. That was the model her Master showed to her at the cross: no self-will, no resentment, and no self-justification. So she waited for God, in His own time, to explain to Mama Sian why she had to marry a future pastor. Meanwhile, she continued to do her best to care for her beloved mother.

Mei Tin also recalled what their premarital counselor at church shared with them regarding a Christian marriage and parenting in this world. He explained,

"The temporal human marriage between an imperfect man and an imperfect woman is a symbol of the eternal perfect marriage between Jesus and His church/body. It is like a training ground for the coming eternal relationship though in different dimensions.

Similarly, the temporal damaged human parenting process is a symbol and training ground for God's children to enjoy His perfect fatherhood forever.

Therefore, whether in marriage or parenting while on earth, lasting commitment is required because God's commitment to those who have welcomed Him is eternal.

Due to the above beliefs, we must try our best to be faithful to our spouse and to our children."

Mei Tin and her fiancé then knew that, for better or for worse, they would commit themselves to each other and to their future children till earthly *death do them part.* They began to understand that it is such a simple commitment that kept couples together; not even the best matched personalities could do so in a damaged world and church. In the fulfillment of such a vow, children would be safe.

"However," the counsellor continued, *"marriage, to a traditional Chinese lady, is for security, identity, and immortalization of the next*

generation through childbirth. Her self-identity is not important or as important as her community's identity. Being matchmade into a good family of equal social standing brings dignity to her parents and clan. Marriage is never seen as an individual affair but for the good of the related community. A noble and wise wife will bring praise to her parents, husband, and parents-in-law. What she thinks and desires is not as important as what is generally agreed to be good for her welfare and that of her extended families, not necessarily nuclear family only.

More liberal post WWII western psychologists and socialists have taken years of social upheaval and chaos in their societies before they went round the circle and have come to the same conclusion via intensive and extensive research. They now purport that, generally, a child growing up with extended family support is safer and more balanced emotionally, physically, mentally, and socially than one who does not; that it is better to have two parents (male and female) living together in the tender childhood years (if no violence endangers lives), even if they quarrel, than to have them separate through divorce."

This explanation made sense to the engaged couple, Cheng and Mei Tin. The child existed because both parents once loved each other. Therefore, when the latter separate permanently and painfully, the child inevitably felt like he or she had been cut into two in loyalty, trust and love. Divorce was like the emotional suicide of a marriage and family. This general observation, however, is generalized as every child and adult often has the resilience to grow up well in spite of broken families. Many may turn out broken though they have had loving homes. God calls adults to personal accountability. Hence, no one needs to blame their parents anymore.

The counselor also reminded them that

"sex, to a woman, since Genesis chapter 3 in the history of the fall of mankind, is seen as a means to please man, not the end desire. She agrees to sexual activities in the hope that he would take care of her long term. However, sex, to a man generally, is an end in itself. He gives in

to the woman's requests in order to have sex. Her body is for his needs to feel good and to reproduce with him. But we do not need to argue about the proof of such conclusions. They are genuine life observations like that of the sage, King Solomon of old."

"What is marriage to a traditional Chinese man?" the counselor posed to them as he stood up to have a cup of water.

Cheng and Mei Ti looked at each other and waited for more words of wisdom and discernment . . .

"Marriage, to him, is to have a wife to call his own, to care and to be cared, to meet his sexual needs, and to form a new family. However, due to the prominence of manhood in Chinese culture, a Chinese man also marries to have a son to prolong the culture and traditions of his ancestral family and clan (usually classified according to surnames). To leave his home in order to allow his new marriage and family to mature is not in his mind, though it was in God's mind at creation. The man's primary loyalty is to his parents and whoever is older than him in his living extended family. The patriarch or matriarch (commonly referred to as the tyrants or dowagers if they are harsh and domineering at home) rule the house and have the last say when there are minor or major disagreements."

However, wiser older men would counsel their sons that if he could not lead his own wife and children so that they live peaceably with their immediate extended family, he will hold him primarily accountable. Poor man. No wonder he has to order his wife around to prove his manhood ever so often!

Order in the community household is from top down, never down up. Mutual submission and tender loving care are alien to the traditional Chinese though central in the teaching of the Bible. Children are meant to be seen but not heard unless their parents are exceptionally open-minded or have been renewed through outside influence through general education and the Bible. Filial piety is the norm.

However, having gone to the other extreme of living with spoilt kids and adults in the twenty-first century world, many parents of today wish that the order to be filial to one's parents could make a come back, but not ancestral worship, of course, as that touches on the eternal spiritual realm rather than the realm of temporal human relationships. We cannot really play with the Creator God of all and not get our hands burnt. The human battle would be tough, though, for which mere human can fight the globalization of ideas and relationships through the media where the definition and parameters of morality and norms have been shifted beyond recognition by those deemed more sane.

Chapter 15

Last Years, Months and Days

Kuala Lumpur 1982

Already using a wheelchair since her previous severe stroke, and accompanied by her maid everywhere she went, Sian felt it timely to shift into Mei Tin's home. This would also give Mei Lan and her husband a long deserved relief. The latter had faithfully cared for her in spite of her busy schedule as a teacher, wife and mother. With little personal belongings, Sian flew to Kuala Lumpur to live with Mei Tin and her husband. Overjoyed that she was with her youngest daughter at last, she quickly adjusted to her new environment. Another local maid was employed and the house was soon filled with jokes and mirth.

In Kuala Lumpur, visits from old Penang church friends eased the transition process though the hectic city culture did not affect Sian much as she seldom went beyond the grounds of the church–cum–school next door. New friends were made from the school canteen operators who frequently brought over freshly cooked lunches for her while her daughter and son-in-law were at work. Chinese anywhere understood the need to honor their elders. Sometimes, when these new friends had family squabbles, they would come to seek Sian's advice. The school caretakers, gardeners, and guards of Indian, Malay, or Chinese origins soon became their friends too. As fellow Malaysians, they had got used to living with one another as neighbors. They naturally felt at home with one another. Nobody seemed to have instructed them to do so. Furthermore, the primary school boys would climb over their adjoining school fence to retrieve a ball or yell for Sian's maid to get it for them. When Mei Tin adopted two friendly dogs, the boys were fascinated and often shared their food with them through the wired fence.

In 1983, Mei Tin had her first baby! The small household rejoiced, and Sian's mood was lifted even more. What a difference it made to the Grandma who was too weak to carry her youngest grandson without help now. As Noel grew into an active toddler, Sian would laugh till her denture dropped when the little boy tried to climb onto her lap and accidentally almost pulled down her sarong (a long Malayan wrap around skirt)!

In March 1986, the family decided to invest in a small house in Gombak instead of pay high rental in the city. Son-in-law Cheng carried Mama Sian into the front seat of their old Honda Civic and drove her to the new place which was not ready for use yet. Sian beamed as she viewed the house from outside but said to them,

"I will not be living here."

"What, Mama?" asked Mei Tin who could not believe her ears.

"I will not be living here," she repeated.

Sensing this could be a taboo subject and not wanting to cause misunderstanding, Mei Tin kept her mother's comment to herself.

True enough, in early May that year, Sian's health suddenly deteriorated rapidly. Mei Tin informed Papa Li and all her siblings as soon as she could. Mei Lan and Papa Ah Li rushed from Penang. Thankfully, Sian could still communicate with them. However, when her daughters urged her to forgive Papa, her mood changed. She refused to eat or talk for a few days. Apparently, the maid overheard Ah Li taunting Sian about his good health and longevity. How cruel! Yet, unless Sian forgave him on her side, peace evaded her. The family prayed for Mama to release Papa and let God deal with him. No one could convict of sin; only the Holy Spirit could.

Following that, to round up a chapter of her past, Mei Tin gently asked her dear Mama,

"Do you now believe that a pastor son-in-law can take care of you?"

Sian nodded and smiled approvingly. How affirming it was for Mei Tin after eight years of marriage to Cheng.

One week later, Sian prayed to forgive Papa and whoever had hurt her in the past. From that moment on, Sian rested in peaceful sleep till God took her home. On a Tuesday dawn, Mei Tin woke up at 6:15 a.m. and checked on her Mama. As she felt her pulse, it was getting weaker for a few seconds and then stopped. Quite often, God gave His believed children time to say good-bye to loved ones before they left this world. Mei Tin saw a vision of angels urging Sian to climb the long and steep stairs to God. Sian did not wait, she just ran up with a final joyful anticipation to meet her Savior! No more dislocated hip, no more limp. She broke into a dance as she reached the top! Mei Tin hugged her pastor husband tightly and wept with a great relief, praying softly,

"Thanks, Father, I am sure You will now explain to Mama why I had to obey You. I know that she will now realize that I did not intentionally hurt her feelings by marrying Cheng! It is just that You have taught me to lovingly obey You above all else."

While the curtain fell on Sian's life on earth,
her children rose to call her
Blessed of the Lord!

Blessings and Transforming Grace

What is a Blessing?

"Her children call her blessed" is the proud refrain which every Chinese woman wants to hear and experience. Sian was one of them. Yes, her friends and neighbors often praised Mama for her seven well behaved children who also excelled in their studies. However, would she count herself blessed? Knowing Sian, I doubt it. Why?

This is because the husband of her youth betrayed her trust. His womanizing habits repeatedly ate into her heart. In spite of his empty words of having only one wife, not two, and that womanizing was only his relaxing flings, she could not be convinced. Which faithful wife would when, for periods now and then, he longed for the other women day and night like a young first time infatuated suitor?

Papa's unrelenting infidelity was the family's main sorrow. Children who grow up in such a family atmosphere commonly feel sad. As for Mei Tin, she did not even realize that till one afternoon, three lady friends and she sat down for tea. They had just attended a conference in Port Dickson, Malaysia. One of them suggested that they could go round answering a question as an exercise so that they could know each other better as they were new friends. They were to use one word or a phrase to describe their individual childhood.

- The first said *"irritable"* as she recalled having been an irritable and restless child.
- The second said *"confused"* as her parents argued a lot and she did not have much parental guidance.
- The third said *"fearful"* as fear of punishment was her motivation to be good and to study well.
- Lastly, Mei Tin said *"sad"* though she had never thought of her past in this way before. But her instant answer made her think and ask herself . . .

"What was in my childhood experiences that caused me to sum them up as sad?"

As she pondered, she began to realize the depth of the wound inflicted by her Papa's betrayal of trust to Mama. All their siblings' childhood sorrows and fears centered around the dilemma and drama from this one fact.

Writing this story at near old age could be therapeutic for Mei Tin. Just two weeks ago, she woke up with a dream that old furniture was flowing out of her. Maybe this is what it was about. God was getting rid of the sad memories lodged in her childhood mind. She must let Him perform this emotional–mental surgery, painful though it might be, if He saw it fit. Only then could she live an even freer and more joyful life that would take her into the golden years of old age!

She once prayed that one day, when she grew up, she would tell all fathers never to betray the trust of their wives, like what her grandfather and father did because they would hurt not only the wife but all their children as well. Is it any wonder that Malachi, an Old Testament prophet, called for fathers to return to their children and children to their fathers (Malachi 4:6).

About four hundred years later, John the Baptist, the forerunner of the Messiah, Jesus, repeated this call in Luke 1:17. Should not this have a significant connotation to all human families and marriages when imprinted into the last book of the Old Testament and the first chapter of the Gospel of Luke the physician, who must have seen much family problems through his medical work? Time will tell. Meanwhile, let the Master speak . . .

What is the meaning of being blessed?
Jesus once taught . . .
"Blessed are the poor in spirit for theirs is the kingdom of heaven.
Blessed are those who mourn for they will be comforted.
Blessed are the meek for they will inherit the earth.
Blessed are those who hunger and thirst for righteousness for they will be filled.
Blessed are the merciful for they will be shown mercy.
Blessed are the pure in heart for they will see God.
Blessed are the peacemakers for they will be called children of God.
Blessed are those who are persecuted because of righteousness for theirs is the kingdom of heaven."

Sian died peacefully in Kuala Lumpur in May 1986. She had fulfilled all the reasons for being blessed! Waiting for Ah Li to cherish her had become irrelevant.
Ah Li died from postoperative complications, after the removal of a cancerous tumor, while he made a final trip to his village in September 1989.
But something happened six months before he died . . .

In traditional Chinese culture, once a daughter is married, her parents no longer make demands on her to support them since she is now accountable to her husband's parents and had to submit to them first. Therefore, when Ah Li needed money for his support, he would approach his sons. However, all three sons refused to give him more than gifts for his birthday and Chinese New Year. They did not want him to squander his resources on his women. So, in old age, he felt deeply rejected by the very sons he thought he could depend on. But they were so fearful of his reprimands if they did not meet his demands that they refused to let him visit their homes. Hence, Ah Li not only lost their financial support, he lost his dignity as a father too. He felt the shame silently though he shared it with his youngest son-in-law, the pastor, once. This was something very hard on a Chinese father. Thankfully, his four daughters and their respective husbands continued to keep in touch with him, gave him some cash, and took him out for his favorite meals whenever they could.

Then, Mei Lan and Mei Tin, the two left in Malaysia, suddenly had an idea. They would celebrate his eightieth birthday (according to Chinese age) for Papa Li. This was a birthday counted auspicious in Chinese custom. Mei Lan's husband also suggested that they make it a bigger do by inviting Papa's peer group old friends and relatives who were still in Penang. Giving Papa the privilege of calling his own friends boosted his dignity of being respected as a father again, especially in the eyes of Chinese fellowmen. The birthday dinner in a grand new five star hotel brought much joy to him to whom the cultural face saving was like saving his life! Neither daughter, however, expected his response in the weeks and months after the celebration.

For about six months, every now and then, Papa Ah Li called up Mei Lan and Mei Tin separately to thank them, profusely and repeatedly, for the honor of the birthday party. The surprise over Ah Li's behavior needs to be understood from the angle of the Chinese culture of honoring one's parents.

As a proud traditional Chinese father, though he loved his children, he was not in the habit of thanking them for anything as he regarded their gifts and obedience as their due to him. Neither was he used to saying *"sorry"* to them when he made mistakes. His word was their command. If he ordered,

"Ah Jin, polish my shoes," Ah Jin must do it there and then. If he were to order,

"Mei Tin, play the piano before my business friends,"

Mei Tin had to put aside whatever she was doing to obey him first. She must also politely greet his friends with a smile, even though she was boiling inside as her own activity had been disrupted without notice. If she obeyed, his friends would praise him for raising such good children. *"Please"* was also not in his vocabulary.

The children learnt to read his approval for them by his facial expressions and tone of voice. Therefore, when he was so expressive of his gratefulness, Mei Tin, being more surprised than her sister, did not know how to answer. She was just so happy that Papa was finally cheerful and jovial again. When he thanked her one more time, Mei Tin finally gathered up her courage and reminded him to return to worship God in the local church. This had been her prayer for him for twenty years after Mama gave up praying for him. It was a quick reminder to him to give thanks to God if he were so happy. Papa replied in the affirmative, and this gave her much peace of mind as she had once heard him complain angrily to Mama when his business was depressingly low,

"How can Jesus be real if my business cannot be rescued!"

After Papa Ah Li died, news reached Mei Lan that a few months before he made his final journey to China, he visited the new and much younger male pastor of his home church, which justly excommunicated him from fellowship over twenty years ago. On discovering that he was not in, he asked to speak to the even younger lady church worker and voluntarily confessed to her, "I have sinned because I took a mistress."

Though Mei Tin was in the dark about whether he really was in God's family before, due to his affair and refusal to apologize to God and to his wife, she was then sure that Papa was God's child as much as anyone in Christ. Furthermore, for a Chinese man to confess his sin to an unknown younger lady church worker was rare and thus made it more convincing that his repentance was real. For Mei Tin, this was God's reward for praying and waiting for over twenty years for her father to repent and be assured of his salvation. A belated answer was still an answer.

Pa's appreciation of grace through a simple birthday party led him to repentance when He discovered afresh how much God had always loved him and given him what he needed. No one else could have known the depth of his pains of rejection by his sons. He then returned to His true Father in peace and joy and to the wife of his youth while on earth! In Malaysia, Mei Tin had a vision of Papa Ah Li running up the stairs to heaven and shouting hilariously . . .

"Heavenly Father, I want to see Sian!"
Papa Li had been . . .
Freed from sin to be reconciled with God and man!
Freed from negative aspects of his human culture to say thanks!
Freed from the old body to receive the new!
Freed from self to behold His face!

One Sunday, when a family friend commented about Papa Li,

"What fear, alienation, and criticism could not do, grace did! Praise the Lord indeed!",

Mei Lan and Mei Tin looked at each other and grinned as they recalled how God used an unexpected birthday feast to help Papa regain his fatherhood and thus understand God's grace, His mercy of which no one is worthy and which no one can earn. It had to be a gift. Thus Papa Li, through the renewal of his mind, was transformed by grace.

"Thanks Heavenly Father, for Your Gift of Transforming Grace!"
Sayonara . . .
I hope you enjoyed reading this book as much as
I enjoyed writing it for you!
Meideli